Athletic Alchemy

Transformation of The Complete Athlete

Donnie Ray Evege

About The Author

Donnie Ray Evege is a sought after motivational speaker, and founder of DEEP Enterprises which is a multitude of businesses and philanthropic work that aims to empower individuals and teams to become the best version they can possibly become.

He is a former Division 1 NCAA student athlete who played football for The Ohio State University, where he and his team won 4 Big Ten Titles, played in the 2008 National Championship and won the 2010 Rose Bowl and the 2011 Sugar Bowl! He was All-Academic Big 10, graduated in 2011 with a Strategic Communication degree, and now travels the world speaking and training on personal development. His tagline rings true for everything that you will encounter in life...which is; *Go Deep Within To Bring Outer Excellence.*

Visit Donnie's website at www.DonnieRayEvege.com

Dedication

We are all students and we are all athletes in this game called *Life*.

This book is dedicated to all the students and athletes that are ready and willing to take their game to a higher level in the classroom, on the field and in their communities.

My goal is to help transcend the mind of the player by learning from my story. To go from acting in Faith instead of fear, and to live out their full potential.

Foreword

"Donnie Evege has always had an intellectual and emotional passion to help others. As a high school student, as an Ohio State Buckeye, and now in his professional life, Donnie seeks to find a way to make a difference FOR OTHERS. Athletic Alchemy will be a terrific resource for students, parents, and young professionals. **A comprehensive plan** for your journey of success, and a game plan to handle the challenges that accompany that path. Proud of you Donnie Evege !!"

JAMES P. TRESSEL
PRESIDENT
Youngstown State University

Introduction

I wrote this book because I wanted to share my journey. Playing football and being a member of the Ohio State Buckeyes taught me valuable lessons that I want to share with the world.

Athletic Alchemy is about enhancing your mindset and encouraging you to go within yourself to develop a personal transformation that's geared towards achieving your dreams.

This book was inspired by my experiences being a student athlete and football player for The Ohio State University. I was blessed to be a part of an amazing team and have an incredible coach that taught priceless life lessons. The lessons I learned as a student athlete at OSU empowered me as an athlete, improved me as a student and stay with me today for life after sports.

As a motivational speaker, I love passing on the torch of empowerment to current students and athletes. This book is for every student athlete, professional athlete, parent of an athlete, and anyone who approaches life with the athletic mentality of victory and success.

My intention in writing this book was to help and encourage you along your journey of sports, education and transitioning into different playing fields.

I know what strategies and thought patterns worked for me, and which ones didn't. If I can help you avoid potential pitfalls and detrimental decisions, then what you hold in your hands can be a valuable resource for you. I care about your mindset and your inner belief system. Use the messages in the pages that follow as ammunition for your own life and as fuel to accomplish whatever you set your mind to.

DEEP
Donnie Evege Empowering Players
Worldwide
Table of Empowerment

Part 1

My Mini Memoir

Chapter 1

The Dream

2007 through 2011 were some of the best years of my life. I entered Ohio State as a freshman student athlete in 2007, and graduated with a Strategic Communication degree in 2011. I had the honor of playing *football* for **The Ohio State Buckeyes**, and the privilege of playing for Hall of Fame Head Coach, Jim Tressel!

When I reflect back, I feel so blessed to have experienced this special journey. Not much compares to running out of the tunnel in front of 105,000+ Buckeye fans, and knowing there are millions more watching!

People often ask me, "What was it like running out of the tunnel onto the field?" And I always respond with, "The feeling's *ELECTRIC*!"

One of the things I cherish the most during my years at Ohio State was the camaraderie with my teammates.

I had so many memorable experiences

with my teammates. The bonds formed from pushing through tough practices and winning championships were priceless experiences that have helped shape who I am today.

I'll talk more about my experiences at Ohio State and a few very special teammates later in the book.

But for now, I'd like to rewind back in time and share with you how I even got to Ohio State my freshmen year in 2007.

My Early Years

It all started where I was born, a small town in Ohio, right outside of Dayton, called Xenia. Dayton is home of the Wright Brothers, home of aviation where flying began. Xenia, on the other hand, is known for its dangerous weather.

I was born into a foundation of *overcoming*. In 1974 an F5 tornado came through Xenia and caused immeasurable heartbreak and damage. But the town and its people overcame.

Like everywhere in America, sports brings people together - especially football. Growing up I played several sports – baseball, basketball, track, football, soccer, even martial arts. It's funny to think back and realize that I was very close to not even playing football. My dad, Donnie Sr., played college baseball. He felt that football was too dangerous for a 3rd grader to participate in. My mom thought otherwise. While my dad was at work, my mom snuck me to my first football practice at Shawnee Elementary School, also known as the "Shawnee Braves."

I'd be remised if I did not talk about how blessed and grateful I am to have my parents in my life. My mom sacrificed so much in order to be there for not only my younger sister, Briana and I, but also all the kids in our community. My dad was also very much involved. He was my very first basketball and baseball Coach as a child, and was a phenomenal role model and mentor to my friends and I. My dad always demonstrated integrity and faith. He led by example and still does to this very day. I am forever grateful for having him as my father!

After we told my dad that I made the team, and after he saw the joy and excitement that I had, and after meeting my youth football coaches, he allowed me to continue playing football.

Photo of my parents and I after winning the 4th grade Superbowl

I was blessed to play for elementary coaches that taught the fundamentals first. Head Coach Ken Phoenix, a.k.a. Coach Hubba, was a coach that did not believe in young athletes hitting every day during practice. He did a great job at teaching the fundamentals of football and emphasizing the importance of character development.

Another coach on my Shawnee Braves football team that I would like to talk about for a moment, is a man who played a key role in helping me excel throughout my athletic career. His name was Booker Washington a.k.a. Coach Buzz. Even as young peewee athletes, he instilled faith in his players. He always helped build and lift us up. He always talked about the importance of getting good grades, treating people with respect, and making good decisions on and off the field.

Coach passed away after a hard fought battle with cancer. But before he passed he made a surprise visit to my house when I was in middle school. He came with a truckload of weights, plates, bars, and benches. He saw a lot of potential that myself, and my two best friends, Ryan and Bryan Simpson had, and wanted to gift and equip us with tools that would take our ability to a higher level.

Coach Buzz never directly said this, but him giving me a weight room spoke to me. And what I intuitively heard was that *athletic ability* is not enough. If I wanted to live out the full potential that he saw in me, I would have to work. So, I would like to take this moment to thank Coach Buzz. Thank you for igniting a flame that turned into a fire passion for working out and a love for training! Coach, thank you.

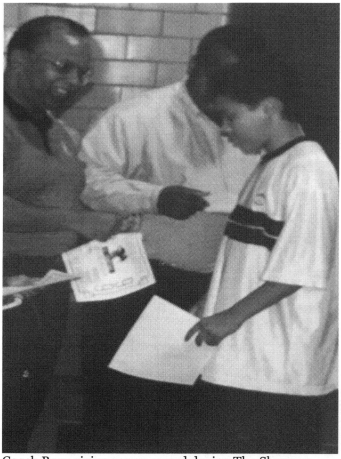

Coach Buzz giving me an award during The Shawnee Braves 4th Grade Football Banquet.

For the next two years Ryan, Bryan and myself trained ferociously! There's a difference between simply working out and training with a purpose. We had a big goal in mind, and we trained constantly with a purpose.

My mom wasn't thrilled about us working out in the living room. Not many parents would be excited to see a bench press and weights take up the majority of space in the living room. Wouldn't you agree?

That small ranch house on Lexington Ave in the east end of Xenia did not present a lot of room. It was tight space with limited room to move. But my parents admired our dedication and wanted to see my goal of playing Varsity football as a freshman come true!

Timeline Of My High School Years:

But first, allow me to highlight some players that came from the Dayton area, and tell you a story that *lit an internal fire*:

Ohio has proven to have some of the best football programs in the country! Dayton has always been known to have outstanding programs of its own.

Football programs like the Centerville Elks produced Buckeye Captain and ESPN Analyst, Kirk Herbstreit. They've also produced one of the best kickers to ever play the game; Ohio State All American, and NFL great, Mike Nugent. They've also produced one of the best linebackers to play at Ohio State, and the #5 pick in 2005 NFL draft, A.J. Hawk! Andy Harmon who played at Kent State and the Philadelphia Eagles. Will Johnson played at West Virginia and went on to play for the Pittsburgh Steelers and the New York Giants. Michael Bennett played for Ohio State and the Jacksonville Jaguars.

Dayton also boasts the number 1 overall

pick in the 1994 NFL Draft, Dan Big
Daddy Wilkerson from Dayton Dunbar
and Keith Byars one of the best running
backs to ever play in Columbus from
Dayton Roth was the number 10 overall
pick in the 1986 draft and went on to
star for the Philadelphia Eagles, Miami
Dolphins, the New England Patriots and
the New York Jets.

Northmont Thunderbirds produced
Ohio State All American and Captain,
Kurt Coleman who has gone on to play
in Superbowl 50 and be nominated for
countless humanitarian awards.
Northmont also produced Ohio State
captain, defensive back C.J. Barnett who
played for the New York Giants. They
also produced a phenomenal
quarterback and overall athlete, Clay
Belton, who went on to play college
football and professionally.

Xenia's Trent Cole is a two time Pro
Bowler who played for the University of
Cincinnati.

Springfield Wildcats always produces
phenomenal talent and is coached by a
University of Kentucky graduate, 12 year
NFL standout and incredible human

being, Maurice Douglas. Coach Douglas is a state champion coach who has literally helped countless guys go to college from his years coaching at Trotwood Madison and now the Springfield Wildcats. Among the many greats to come out of Springfield is Dee Miller! Dee Miller was a tremendous athlete and playmaker for the Buckeyes, and also played for the Green Bay Packers.

That's just to name a few of the players that the GWOC (Greater Western Ohio Conference) has produced.

This quick story begins with me confiding and talking with a teacher/coach at my middle school after class. I expressed to him that the following year I was considering attending other high schools that offered more athletic and academic opportunities to their student athletes.

His exact words were, "Donnie, if you leave, you'll just be a small fish in a big pond. But if you stay, you'll be a big fish in a small pond."

He shook his head and basically told me

that I wouldn't make it at any other school except for Xenia.

Even though I was at an impressionable age, I had a pretty strong mind.

But in all honesty, hearing his opinion and limited belief in me, hurt.

I made the decision to keep his words near and dear to my heart. He didn't know it, but he lit an internal fire within me that motivated me.

Moving forward, I had to sort out my feelings and put together a game plan.

I had to first honor my emotions. I allowed myself to feel the disappointment that came from hearing someone who I once looked up to, essentially say that I wasn't good enough to compete at a bigger school on a bigger stage. The next emotion I felt was a mix of anger and pride.

I had to make the decision to not accept my teacher's limited opinion of me. I had big dreams of being a top student athlete and playing at the highest levels that my God given talent, and work ethic could take me!

Instead of accepting my teacher's opinion of me, **I embraced the fuel his words evoked and purposefully channeled energy towards being the best overall student athlete that I possibly could become**.

I was dedicated to tapping into my fullest potential and creating a vision that was a lot bigger than any "pond" metaphor.

Because of him, I set my vision beyond local ponds and fish. Internally, I was planning and training to be a shark dominating the ocean. And with that internal drive, I did something that changed my career forever!

The Power of the Pen

With an internal fire lit, wanting to prove the non believers wrong and motivated to be the best that I could possibly be...I did something my dad always told me held great power.

That was to goal set with a purpose.

Still in the 8th grade, I sat down at the kitchen table and listed every single goal I wanted to accomplish during my high school years. Goals pertaining to my grades (quarterly G.P.A's, core G.P.A's, A.C.T scores), training goals in the weight room I wanted to accomplish, speed and agility goals, spiritual goals and even financial goals.

I really put a lot of time and energy into deciding what I envisioned and what I wanted to accomplish. I wrote "in depth goals" for each year of the four years that followed.

After writing my last goal, I signed and dated my goal sheet.

I took it a step further and had my dad read what I had written. I asked him to sign it as a witness, and he did. To show you how serious I was about achieving my goals, I asked my dad to also sign and date his dad's name, *Bobby Ray Evege* who passed away in 1999 as a special, honorary witness.

I was focused and determined!!

Deep Questions/Reflections

Have you ever had someone try to limit you?

Have you ever had someone not believe in your vision and dreams?

If you could go back in time a week, a month or years; what encouraging advice would you give your younger self?

Always remember that other people's opinion of you does not have to be the opinion you have of yourself. You have the freedom to choose your attitude, perspective and the direction you go in life.

You can begin right now to form a new and better belief system. **You have purpose and YOU will become the best version of YOURSELF.**

Pay Up

I want to take you back in time and
share with you a quick story that
transpired in 2002. The same year Ohio
State beat the Miami Hurricanes in the
National Championship, and one year
before my internal flame got lit by my
8th grade teacher.

When I was in the 7th grade my dad took
a small group of guys and myself to visit
Ohio State's campus to meet a college
counselor.

The purpose of this visit was to have a
meeting with an academic advisor at the
college level to discuss the importance of
education, taking our grades seriously,
and to get a feel of what the possibilities
were. Additionally we needed to
understand the potential of what our
future could be if we continued to
succeed in the classroom and on the
field.

I'll never forget what Mr. James Hall
impressed upon me. In relation to
academics, sports training, and in life he
said, **"You'll either pay now or
you'll pay later…. but no matter**

what, you're going to pay." Those words carry so much value and truth. Whether you're a 7th grader reading this book right now or a corporate executive, this truth remains the same. If you have a deadline whether it's a high school reading assignment, writing a paper for a college English Literature class or developing a marketing presentation for your Sr. Vice President, you can either procrastinate or execute good time management skills and do the work. If you want to be successful, you have to put in the time and energy it takes in order to do so.

DEEP Questions/Reflections

Do you oftentimes find yourself waiting until the last minute to finish homework?

Do you put studying off until the last minute and cram the night before a test?

We all have procrastinated at times. The key is to know yourself, and know your struggles.

If you struggle with procrastination then you need to ask yourself, ***are the goals I've set worth me prioritizing my time better and doing the work in advance?***

The solution here is to practice good time management skills. Prioritize your schedule and put first things first.

In order to be successful at any level you have to become a person who executes great time management skills.

I'll repeat the advice that Mr. James Hall gave me my 7th grade year.

You'll either pay now or you'll pay later...but no matter what, you're going to pay.

What does achieving your goals and dreams cost? Are you willing to pay the price?

You have it within you to buy it!

I'll talk more about what achieving your goals take later in the book when we discuss, *The Intangibles.*

Chapter 2

Timeline Of My High School Years

2003: Leading into my 9th grade year I attended The Ohio State three day football camp. I was the second fastest camper there, running a 4.51 forty yard dash.

Having a great overall camp, making a good first impression on the coaching staff and running a fast 40 time really put me on the radar.

9th grade season: I accomplished my goal! I earned a starting position on my varsity football team as a freshman! I played for a great head coach, Paul Jenne.

I also played JV basketball, ran varsity track and maintained a 3.8 G.P.A.

The next summer 2004 leading into my sophomore year I attended The Ohio State three day football camp for the second year in a row. This time around, I had the fastest 40 yard dash time at the camp, clocking in at 4.35

I also attended the Notre Dame football camp. For the second camp in a row and among 300 other campers, I was the fastest camper there. I met the coaching staff and left such an impression that the head football coach, Tyron Willingham let me know that if I were to go to Notre Dame and play for him, I'd have the opportunity to run for class president, join a fraternity and play baseball!

After running a 4.35 at OSU, being the fastest athlete at Notre Dame and having a solid season on varsity as a freshmen, more colleges began to take notice.

I was excited and looking forward to my sophomore year at Xenia High School.

Then, not so good news broke. My head coach at the time, Paul Jenne, accepted a new head coaching job at Hillard Darby in Hillard, Ohio. Knowing he was not going to be my coach my sophomore season hurt, but I was genuinely happy for him and his family. The Xenia school district had a levy on the ballot that would potentially cut coaching and teaching jobs. Coach did what any smart person would do and accepted a great position before the possibility of being cut became a reality.

Coach Jenne and I had a good player/coach relationship and it felt like our time together was just getting started.

What happened next took faith, risk and courage to overcome.

2005: To make a long story short, I played my sophomore football season for the new head coach of the Xenia football team. After the football season, my parents decided to move our family to Huber Heights. We decided that the following school semester we would move and transfer to Wayne High School.

Respond With Faith

My father called the Xenia coach and informed him that we were moving. The next day when I saw the coach he told me: "It won't work out for you there!"

My response was, "Coach, if I have God in my life, everything will work out." Then I walked away, *for good.*

What I learned was that it can be tough to make big decisions. It's also tough to transition into unknown territory. But fear not. Always know within yourself that when you have faith, and God on your side, everything will work out.

And everything would work out...

January 15, 2005:

New Guy at a New School,

I'm officially a Wayne Warrior

Being at my new school, I continued to excel as an athlete and experienced even more opportunity with a phenomenal coaching staff led by Coach Jay Minton. Due to the rich tradition at Wayne High School, college coaches always evaluate and look at athletes coming from the program. Former standout guys like

- Buckeye and NFL great, *Will Allen*

- Buckeye captain and now D1 college football coach, *Marcus Freeman*
- Buckeye wide receiver, *John Hollins*
- *Bowling Green wide receiver, Ronnie Redd*
- *Bowling Green and NFL* wide receiver, *Robert Redd*
- Miami of Ohio defensive tackle, *Martin Channels*
- West Virginia offensive lineman, *Jeff Burk*
- Cincinnati Bearcat, NFL Cornerback and Bowling Green Corners Coach, *Mike Mickens*
- Purdue wide receiver and former NFL player, *Greg Orten*
- Cincinnati Bearcat wide receiver and Wayne football Coach, *Roosevelt Mukes*
- *Michigan State defensive tackle and NFL player, Jerel Worthy*
- and Buckeye record holder, two-time Big 10 player of the year, freshman player of the year, and NFL great, *Braxton Miller*

all graduated from Wayne High School. I could write an entire book listing the phenomenal high school and college athletes that came out of Wayne! Playing for Head Coach Jay Minton and his incredible staff of assistant coaches put me in an advantageous position to have the opportunity to play football at the next level.

As soon as I stepped foot on the Wayne High School campus I was greeted with welcoming arms. My classmates, teammates, coaches and community at large were awesome people!

I immediately got involved. I ran indoor track under the guidance of Hall of Fame Head Track Coach, Mike Fernandez a.k.a. Coach Fern. Coach Fern helped me tremendously with my running form and technique that would soon help me break my personal best forty yard dash record later that summer.

I immediately saw the benefits of being around a coaching staff and groups of people who had a championship mindset. Everyone, and I mean everyone worked hard. The coaches taught Warrior pride and did a phenomenal job in instilling discipline in the whole team...

especially the seniors.

Coach Minton, Coach Fern and the entire staff knew the importance of building leadership and accountability in the upperclassman. Coaches instilled in us the importance of leading by example, encouraging the underclassman and taking each training session and study table seriously. I was always reminded that my training in the weight room and in the classroom would not only benefit me on the field, but also in life. I'm forever grateful to all the coaches for instilling in me what all young people need. That discipline and work ethic always trumps talent and athletic ability!

I decided to take my academic success into my own hands by registering to take the A.C.T. my sophomore year. There was a lot of material on the test that I had not yet been taught, but I studied and wanted to get acclimated. It was a valuable experience taking the A.C.T early. I learned the style of the test and the stress involved by taking the real thing.

I signed up to take the test again my sophomore year. When I got the results back, I found out that I received a 21 score. Coupled with my gpa, that was a solid score and several points over what many division 1 colleges required for acceptance.

I was blessed to have my dad, and Coach Minton's support in encouraging me to take the test even though I was a sophomore. There are pros to taking initiative early. **Don't wait to do things later that can be accomplished now.** That is my advice to any student athlete reading this. You can take the A.C.T and S.A.T as many times as you can during your high school career. They only take your top scores so there is no risk.

Summer 05
After experiencing the National Indoor Track Championship meet in Maryland, the National Outdoor Track Championship track meet in California, and the State track meet at Jessie Owens Stadium with my teammates and coach Fernandez, I immediately went to the Miami of Ohio football camp with my dad and Coach Minton. With no rest

after competing in the State track meet,
I was clocked running a 4.31 and a 4.32
forty yard dash, back to back. Immediate
college scholarship offers began to
come. A few weeks later I tested a 40'
inch vertical jump in front of my future
strength and conditioning coach, Eric
Licther and Speed Coach, Butch
Reynolds at Ohio State.

I was no longer just on the radar.

Schools were offering me full ride
scholarships. The recruitment process
was beginning to go to a higher level
after my sophomore camp leading into
my junior year.

Fall 05

After training, practicing and preparing
with my new teammates, I was ready to
take the field! My first official season as
a Wayne Warrior went great. We won a
lot of games and made it to the third
round, regional finals of the playoffs. I
was physically confident and ready to
continue on the journey!

I'd like to take this opportunity to share
with you a very special story that was
inspired by a very special man. This
legacy story should encourage you to go
deep within yourself so you can bring
outer excellence to your team.

This story is titled,
The Alex Ritchie Key To The Weight Room Award

Wayne demanded results. And the best
way to get results is by preparing in the
off-season. Coaches are always
observing who the leaders and hardest
workers are on the team. A man who
exemplified what it meant to be a Wayne
Warrior football player was Alex Ritchie.
He was always one of the hardest
workers, a team player and a leader on
and off the field.

During the 2005 team banquet I was honored by receiving the prestigious award named after Alex. *"The Alex Ritchie Key To The Weight Room Award."*

Alex Ritchie was born on February 13th, 1986 and passed away from a tragic car accident June 6th, 2005. He was a recent Wayne High School graduate and was attending Sinclair Community College while working and giving back at the YMCA. I never had the privilege of meeting Alex, but through hearing Coaches and former players tell stories about his desire to be a leader, hard worker, and through talking with his mother, Mrs. Diana Ritchie and his sister Taylor (Ritchie) on facebook, Alex inspires me everyday to give my best.

His passion for training like a Warrior and lifting other people up, is one of the many special reasons Alex's legacy will always live on.

DEEP Questions/Reflections

Ask yourself this question. What do I want my legacy to be?

Among other special things, Alex Ritchie's legacy was always being a hard worker, caring teammate and leader on the field and in his community.

Are you giving, "Key To The Weight Room Award" effort and dedication to your team or organization?

If not, why?

What things do you need to change or erase from your life that will help you become a better student athlete and overall person?

Begin to Live Your LEGACY Now. Ask yourself, am I giving my absolute best effort in my training? Can I give more to my craft? Remember this fact: The more improvements you get and better results you deliver equals more opportunity for you to showcase your athletic ability. Do the thing that athletic ability does not require, which is, **PREPARE**.

Words of Wisdom

Coach Tressel would often remind the
team that *you can't win a championship
in the off season, but you sure can lose
one.*

Coach Tressel knew there were no
games to be played during winter
conditioning, spring football, or during
2 a day training camp. But he knew that
teams who did not train on a
championship level during the entire
off-season months, did not stand a
chance at winning a championship.

The entire Buckeye team bought into
Coach Tressel's philosophy. We not only
competed against each other during off-
season training, we also competed
against ourselves. We held ourselves and
one another to high standards,
consistently.

Diving all in to coach Tressel's belief
system is the main reason why the teams
I was a part of won 4 Big Ten
Championships.

In order to win big, the entire team has
to be ALL IN.

It begins with you!

What can you do to help your team be **ALL IN** and commit to your team's philosophy?

I'll tell you one thing you can immediately do. You can demonstrate leadership skills by consistently showing up and adding value to your program.

All any teammate, coach or teacher can ask is for you to give your best effort.

Are you giving your best effort in the weight room and in the classroom?

If you are, that's great! But realize you can't win games by yourself. Go uplift and encourage your teammates to step their game up. The coaches play a major role in the success of any team. But always remember, coaches can't play for you.

Your team will only go as far as the leadership standards you set!

What standards do you want to uphold your team?

What standards do you *need* to uphold yourself to?

2006: I continued to train relentlessly during the off-season. I decided not to run track that year so I could focus more energy on weight room training.

During my 2006 school year I was accepted into The National Honor Society. Being a part of the National Society is not easy. You have to maintain a high G.P.A., participate in community service and demonstrate through other requirements why you should be accepted.

I was most proud that I set the goal, accomplished it and made my family and friends proud also.

Being a part of the National Honor Society, having letters of recommendations from teachers and staff, already taking and passing the A.C.T helped my stock rise in recruitment. College coaches would come from across the country to visit Wayne High School. It was great to hear Coach Minton introduce my teammates and I to coach after coach and tell them about what his players were accomplishing in the classroom, in the community and on the field. Coach Minton would often express our resume to college recruiters in that order.

1. Classroom resume. Which is a direct reflection of how well a player is "coachable."
2. Community outreach resume. This is usually a direct reflection of a player's attitude and mindset and character.
3. Lastly, field performance resume backed with statistics and film.

Ohio State offers me a Full Ride Scholarship

The NCAA allows college programs to practice for three to four weeks during the Spring season. During this time, a lot of coaches have open practices for media, recruits and high school coaches to visit campus and watch.

Coach Minton and I took a visit to Columbus to watch Ohio State practice. While Coach Minton and I are in the indoor Woody Hayes Facility we were watching guys warm up and stretch before walk-throughs.

It's a special energy being in the Ohio State "state of the art" facility!

We see Coach Jim Tressel and meet to shake hands around the 50 yard line in the middle of the field. Both coaches greet each other with a smile and chat for a bit.

As Coach Minton and Coach Tressel talk, I can't help but feel like this place is home. Everything about Ohio State is special. But what makes Ohio State great in my opinion, is the people!

Legendary coach Woody Hayes said it best. *"You win with people."*

Leadership comes from the top down. With that said, you won't find a better leader and human being than current Youngstown State President, and my Head Coach, Jim Tressel.

Back to the story: Coach Tressel and I begin to talk a little more in depth. After touching base for a while, it was time for practice to begin. As Coach Tress thanks Coach Minton and I for coming to practice, we shake hands and he says,

"Donnie, we'd love to have you here."

As Coach Tress jogs away to lead practice, Coach Minton and I walk to the end zone. As we're walking Coach Minton looks at me and says, "Next time Coach says *we'd love to have you here,* you respond with, "Coach is that an offer?"

DeJaVu

A week later Coach Minton and I visited Ohio State's open practice. It was almost identical to the previous week's visit. We watched the team warm up and met to shake hands with Coach Tressel around the 50 yard line. After talking for a few moments, Coach Tressel had to leave to lead practice. But before he did, he said the same words. As we shook hands he said, "Donnie, we'd love to have you here."

Remembering the advise Coach Minton gave me, I smiled and responded with,

"Coach, is that an offer?"

Coach Tress looked me square in the
eyes and replied,

"You bet that's an offer. It doesn't matter
what position you play, you're the kind
of guy we want! The official offer will be
in the mail soon."

Have you ever been in an intense
moment and time seemed to slow down?
That's what that special moment felt
like!

It was a surreal moment as Coach
Tressel jogged away to lead his team in
practice.

Coach Minton looked at me with a calm
but yet excited smile, patted me on the
back and said, "congratulations!"

While walking to the end zone I knew
that my life was changed, forever.

News Flash!

I'd be remissed to not go into more detail and explain what high school, college and NFL coaches look for in an athlete during recruitment. This is especially true for college coaches because of the amount of money involved and people's jobs are on the line.

Ask yourself this one simple question.

Am I an *asset*, or am I a *liability*?

Let's dissect what the words asset and liability mean.

In essence, an *asset* is something that appreciates in value, while a *liability* has potential risk.

A coach has to trust you. He has to have confidence that you'll make good decisions off the field and that you're prepared for game day, both physically and mentally.

If you're in high school getting recruited, you are now being viewed as an *investment*. College is very expensive.

Division 1 college football programs only have a limited number of full ride athletic scholarships that they can give out each year to incoming freshmen.

So, why should a college coach invest in you? Be honest with yourself. Have you consistently proven that you have the work ethic, dedication and desire to add value to a college program? If so, that's fantastic. If not, what's holding you back from being the best student athlete you can be? You're on limited time. Four years of high school flies by!

R.O.I.

College programs that invest in multi million dollar facilities and over a $100,000 dollar scholarship expect a R.O.I.

R.O.I. stands for *return on investment.*

The best way for you to make it to the next level is to first prove to your current high school coaches that you have what it takes. They're the ones who have relationships with the college coaches, and they're the voices and opinions the college recruiters listen to.

If a player shows major signs they're a liability for their high school/college program, it's simply, on to the next athlete. No "one" player is irreplaceable. It doesn't matter how great of a player you think you are, you can be replaced. Knowing this should encourage you to always bring your A game everyday on the field and off the field!

DEEP Questions/Reflections

Look within and make the necessary changes so you can position yourself for success at the next level.

I tell you the times I ran and the grade point average I maintained not to impress you, but to impress upon you the potential outcomes that can happen when you work hard, train smart and ultimately position yourself for success.

Coach Minton is exactly right when he tells his players that *it all starts in the classroom.* You can't be a great game day player who does just barely enough in the classroom to be eligible. Your goal should be the best and highest version of yourself possible. You should strive and work towards being the smartest and best student you can be. Leaving no untapped potential behind involving your education.

Take your grade point average more seriously than your speed and strength numbers!

You can run blazing fast 4.2, 4.3 and 4.4 forty yard dash times and not give yourself the opportunity to even be accepted into college because you have a poor G.P.A. You can't be just a fast guy with a zero football I.Q. You need to be well rounded and excel in every area.

It all starts in the classroom. If you can't be coachable in the classroom you can't be coachable on the field.

-Jay Minton-

Control what you can control. YOU most certainly can control how you use your time. We are all on an equal playing field in respect of time. We each get 24 hours in a day.

The empowering thing is you get to choose what you give your energies to.

What are you focused on mentally?

How much time and attention are you giving things that you shouldn't be focusing on?

My advice to you is, **"Don't major in minor things."**

A high school football player recently asked me what my advice was on dealing with distractions? My response was that **your goal and vision has to be more important and outweigh any distraction or temptation that comes your way.**

Distractions come and go. But once you begin to give in and feed distractions with your time and energy, they have a way of staying. They can begin to stay in your life longer than what you had ever thought possible. They then begin to blur your *visions* of your future.

They can then transform into something

else. HABITS. And we all know what habits can become. Habits shape your destiny.

So, take anything or anyone that "distracts" you from obtaining your goal and being the best version of yourself, extremely seriously. Always be the BEST YOU that YOU can be!

Be non-negotiable with anything that compromises who you want to become.

Summer 2006: I made the decision that I wanted to graduate high school a semester early, so I could be an early enrollee at Ohio State. In order to me enroll into Ohio State during Spring Quarter 2007, I'd have to plan my class schedule accordingly and make sure my credits met all the requirements that high school and college requires. There are a lot of things that have to happen for a student to graduate early. That is why I encourage players to form a good relationship with their guidance counselors. Always check and double check to make sure your transcripts and credits meet the standards months in advance.

I'd train with my high school team early in the morning for summer workouts, and then make a quick 15 minute drive to Vandalia Butler High School where I took the 2nd semester of my American Government class.

It was worth the sacrifice of going to bed extremely early and studying during the day to accomplish my goal of being able to graduate a semester early in January.

Summer school was a success. I got an A in the class.

Training at this point was going phenomenal! The whole team pushed each other and trained tirelessly.

I remember my teammate and close friend, Joe Gilford and I pushing one another to our limits! We had one goal in mind: to be the strongest physically and mentally we could be so we'd be at our best for our final season at Wayne. Guys like Joe Gilford and defensive back, Keith Dixon represent what a program like Wayne is all about. They uplift their teammates, accept guys like myself who were new to the program and take pride in what the jersey represents.

Our motto our senior was, *Together We Will.* We'd break down every practice with that saying. Together everyone achieves more. As you continue to read on, think of ways you can bring your team or organization closer together. Think of ways you can demonstrate leadership and create a winning work environment the way Joe, Keith and Wayne leadership did in the weight room and field environment.

Fall 2006: Similar to my junior season, my senior year we won a lot of games and made the state playoffs.

We lost to Cincinnati Sycamore in a hard fought game in the 1st round of the playoffs. After hugging my teammates and coaches in the locker room, I took a moment to reflect back.

So much had transpired in my life for me to be in the position I was in, in that moment. The sacrifices my family had made so I could be a Wayne Warrior.

I thought about Ryan, Bryan and many of my childhood friends and teammates

I played with growing up.

I thought about the love and support that the Huber Heights community showed me.

Even though we lost a hard fought playoff game, in that moment, in that locker room:

I was grateful for all that I had been blessed to experience.

Later that night once I arrived home, it hit me. I realized that I only had a little over one month left of high school.

It would take all the lessons that I had learned up to that point, and a focused mindset to prepare me to handle what was to come.

January 2007: I'm now an early graduate of Wayne High School.

I would officially be enrolled at Ohio State and begin practicing with the football team in April. This left me a solid 3 months to get ready!

During the time from being finished with high school and going to college, I did a couple things.

First: I stuck to a strict training and diet program. Preparation is always key, and I wanted to be in the best physical condition entering Ohio State.

Second: I wanted to get my real estate license. I enrolled in Hondros College and took classes so I could get certified to get my real estate license.
I was on a very similar schedule as my summer training and 2nd semester of Government during summer school.

I was pretty busy with working out and going to Hondros College. But I did have free time during the three month wait. I was able to spend valuable time with family and close friends before my new journey began.

Time flew by and before I knew it, it was time for me to say goodbye...

I am officially a Buckeye! O-H!

Chapter 3

Our Journey
Timeline Of My College Years, 2007-2011.

Here are highlights of impactful events that occurred during my first year as a Buckeye, along with DEEP Reflection/Question.

During my time in college I experienced success and setbacks. There were times I was a starter and feeling great! And there were times I was injured and on the bench. I suffered three season ending injuries that presented unique adversity.

As you read my college timeline and short stories, think about your life, and how you can apply lessons learned from my experiences, in your life.

I hope my mini memoir and timeline helps you in some way along your personal journey!

Spring April 2007: Arriving on Ohio State's campus as an early enrollee was a big deal. I was sacrificing a lot in hopes of reaping rewards by being proactive with my education and athletic career.

I had three goals in mind when I decided to enroll early. I wanted to

1. Get a jumpstart academically and earn college credits.
2. I wanted to get acclimated to college campus and college life.
3. And the main reason why I wanted to enroll early was to gain *competitive advantage.*

I concluded that the advantages of me graduating high school a semester early, and enrolling in college Spring quarter would put me in a better position of achieving my athletic and academic goals vs. arriving when most freshmen normally do.

DEEP Reflection

I'm glad I made the decision to enroll at OSU early. You'll read more about the ups and downs of my college journey here shortly.

College presents its unique challenges to everyone. But there are greater challenges to a young person who sacrifices half of their senior year to embark on a journey of a lifetime!

If you're a high school student athlete who is considering going to college early, I would challenge you to ask yourself some questions. Ask yourself, *why*?

What are the deep reasons you want to graduate high school early and enroll in college?

Ask yourself if you're mature enough to handle the responsibility of being on your own away from home?

Lastly, I'd recommend you get a sheet of paper and draw a straight line down the middle. On the left side wright "Pro's" and on the right side write, "Con's."

Make a list of both the pros and cons regarding enrolling into college early.

After you've taken time to do the written exercise, go over what you've written with a trusted person. Ask a mentor if he or she would meet with you to help you evaluate a major decision in your life.

At the end of the day whatever you choose to do is your decision. Seek wise counsel and make the decision that's best for you.

Spring April 2007: It felt incredible to finally be on the team and meet my teammates! All the guys looked out for me and played a role in making my transition from high school to college a success.

The college *routine* was the biggest difference from high school to college. Often times my day began at 5 a.m. I was a full time student with a full class load. I had to experience many times being lost on campus and not knowing where exactly to go.

The speed of the game was a lot faster! Every guy was "the man" on their high school team, so the competition was always high. Only the best athletes from around the country make it to a program like, Ohio State.

Every practice and every play meant something. Every play means something at every level...but at Ohio State, it means more. Thinking about all the GREATS that wore the scarlet and grey jersey makes every player want to uphold the winning tradition and the brand that Ohio State Football represents!

The pressure to perform and make plays can propel you to step up, or it can overwhelm you and cause you to think too much. *The way you handle pressure is a direct reflection of your preparation.* And at Ohio State we not only had the best training facilities to train, we also had the best strength and conditioning staff to prepare us!

Thank You Tribute

Two of my coaches that I'd like to take a moment to thank are, *former Assistant Head Strength Coach*, Doug Davis, and *former Head Speed Coach*, Butch Reynolds.

Coach Doug Davis left a remarkable impact on me as a player and as a person. Coach Davis not only pushed his players to their physical limits, he also had a way of enhancing our mental limits as well.

There were plenty of times that coach would go out of his way to encourage me while I was overcoming injuries and rehabbing to get back on the field. His words and time spent coaching me lifted my spirit!

Coach Davis passed away in 2015. He is deeply loved and missed.

Coach Butch Reynolds was a coach that I always looked forward to seeing. He has a special gift of making everyone around him better. I learned a lot about speed and condition training from the world record holder and the former fastest man alive. But I learned even more about how to be a man of high character and how to thrive through life's adversities. Coach Butch Reynolds, thank you for not only being a coach and mentor, thank you for also being a friend!

Photo of my parents, and Butch Reynolds holding me as a baby. Who would have thought that 17 years later he'd be my Speed Coach at OSU? Photo credit to my uncle, Floyd Thomas.

Fall 2007: After experiencing Spring football practice, summer conditioning and 2-a-day camp, it was almost time for the 2007 season to kick off! I was excited and ready to play.

The time came when position coaches met with freshmen to discuss if they would play that season or get redshirted.

I didn't know what to expect.

I wasn't in the two deep depth chart. There was a tremendous amount of upper class talent. Guys like, Malcolm Jenkins who would later win the *Jim Thorpe Award* which is given to the best Defensive Back in the country, and be drafted in the 1st round and win a Superbowl with the New Orleans Saints, Donald Washington who would later be drafted to the Kansas City Chiefs and Chimdi Chekwa who would later be drafted to the Oakland Raiders... were several players that were ahead of me.

After talking with my position coach he informed me that I would Redshirt.

I wasn't thrilled about being redshirted at first. A lot of player's initial thoughts when told they are being redshirted are, "does this mean I'm not good enough to play?" The answer to that question is, you are good enough to play. Reasons for being Redshirted could be you need more development and that extra year of eligibility would benefit you and the team, greatly. Another reason is the depth chart is deep and you wouldn't play much, if at all your freshmen season.

Remember, once a student athlete steps on the field and plays a single play, that is considered a season played. A student athlete gets four years of eligibility. When Redshirted, that athlete still practices and participates with the team. The only thing that's different is on "game-day" you can't play.

The Pros to Being Redshirted

After talking with some of my teammates who were once Redshirted, and several players who wished they had been Redshirted their freshmen year, I felt better about my situation. The best way to look at being Redshirted is you get an extra year to develop in the weight room and on the field, you get to study and learn the playbook more. You will be on scout team and have the opportunity everyday in practice to go against the 1st string players while you help prepare them for the opponent that week, and you also get an extra year of education paid for since you'll still have four years of eligibility after your Redshirt year.

Adversity Strikes (Round 1)

Things were going well. Yes, I very much wanted to play on Saturdays in front of 105,000 Buckeye fans but that wasn't my role quite yet. I accepted my role and took pride in helping the first string offense get better every week. Being on scout team I had to guard the nation's best wide receivers everyday. I felt like my skills at cornerback were getting better and better every practice after guarding NFL caliber receivers such as Brian Robiskie, Brian Hartline, Dane Sazenbacker and the lightening quick, Ray Small.

I was already envisioning myself playing next season. I knew I was ready to line up against any receiver. I had the best outlook on my situation and used my time wisely. I wasn't exactly where I wanted to be, but I was going to maximize every opportunity to get there.

"Have the best outlook and use your time wisely. You may not be exactly where you want to be. How are you going to maximize every opportunity to get there?"

Donnie Ray Evege

Unique Accident

Coach Tressel would always express the importance of special teams, and how the most important play in football was the punt.

Just like I strived to make the 1st team offense better, I wanted to make the starters on special teams better, also.

I was the defensive end on scout team punt return. On this particular play it was my job to rush and try to block the punt. I still remember the play. Unfortunately, I remember the pain I felt even more.

I was in a three point stance lined up on the right edge.

This photo captures my teammate and I getting ready to rush the edge to block the punt.

I got an explosive jump as soon as the football was snapped to kicker, A.J Trapasso. I remember getting in the backfield so quick, unblocked and seeing

A.J. fumble the football. A.J. quickly picked up the football and rushed to kick it, trying to get the ball off before being blocked. While trying to kick the football, A.J. and I collided. His leg kicked my upper shin/lower knee!

I laid on the ground in excruciating pain. My teammate Nate Oliver, came over to check on me. While in the fetal position and holding my knee I said, "It's just a deep bruise."

Nate held his hand out to help me up, but when I tried to put pressure on my leg to stand up, the pain intensified and pulled me directly back down.

The trainers came on the practice field and carted me off the field. While driving off the outdoor field and through the indoor field to reach the athletic training room, all I could do in that moment was put my hands over my face, lean over and cry. The tears I shed were mainly because of the physical pain I was experiencing in that moment. Up until that point, I had never felt that much pain before in my life. But I was also crying because, well, I was simply overwhelmed.

After the team doctor, Dr. Kaeding
pushed and pulled on my leg to see what
hurt and what didn't, he quickly came to
a conclusion. He suspected I had
suffered a torn PCL.

This would be my first taste of injury at
the college level.

A few days later I went to my MRI
appointment. The results showed that I
had a full, level 3 PCL tear, partial MCL
tear and a torn meniscus. I didn't know
much about posterior cruciate ligament
tears. A lot of PCL tears happen in car
compression accidents due to the high
impact of the knee hitting the glove
compartment. A.J. Trapasso kicks the
football with such force that while he
was in the NFL, he hit the jumbotron in
the Dallas Cowboy's stadium.

This was a major setback for me. PCL's
have to heal on their own, over time. I'd
have to rely solely on my physical
therapy and faith to experience a full
recovery.

My journey would be long and oftentimes, lonely. While the team practiced, I was in the training room doing rehab and learning how to walk again. While the team travelled to away games, I was back home watching it on TV.

Injuries affect a players mental state more than the physical state. But just like the saying goes,

"Tough times don't last, but tough people do."

I didn't always feel strong during my journey. But through prayer and a strong support system, I was able to persevere through the tough times.

And so can you.

Old Wounds Need Healed.

Fall 2008: After having undergone minor surgery to clean up the meniscus tear and months of rehab to heal the PCL tear, I felt ready. Or so I thought.

It was now the 2008 season and we were into week three. We were getting ready to play on the road in California vs USC.

That week during practice I had a meeting with the team doctors to look at my knee. I had a noticeable "limp" when I ran that began to get progressively worse during two-a-day camp.

After the doctors examined my knee, they came back with news that I did not want to hear. They told me that I had come back too early and that my quad needed more extensive rehab. The quad muscle protects the knee, and mine was still atrophied and not at a strong enough point to play at the level I needed.

How long would I have to sit and do more rehab? The rest of the season!

Receiving this news was beyond

frustrating. This would be my second year not being able to play or practice due to injury.

At times I would think to myself, "will I ever be the same player?"

The answer was, no.

I would not come back the same player.

I would come back even *better*!

After the doctors gave me the news week three vs USC, the rest of 2008 was dedicated to rehabbing. I lived in the training room and weight room with the team trainers and strength staff. I got stronger and gained a few pounds. Away from doing leg extentions and quad work, I was limited to upper body workouts. My teammates who had once experienced similar injuries as me, warned me that I'd get a lot stronger and gain more muscle mass on my upper body. They were right. I took out a lot of the frustration on the weights! This is a healthy outlet that I wish I would have chosen to do later in my career when more adversity would strike.

I rehabbed the entire season while still encouraging my team. We ended the season with a 10-3 record, being named Big Ten Champs and making an appearance in the Fiesta Bowl vs the Texas Longhorns.

Here's a recap of 2009:

I'm fully healthy and a starter on special teams! It felt amazing playing in Ohio Stadium in front of all the fans, and being an impact player for my team!

I tied a school record with 5 kickoff tackles in a single game. Buckeye fans nickname me, "Little Polamalu" because they say we resemble one another and the long hair connection.

One of **four** Kick Off tackles vs Illinois September 26th, 2009.

I led the team with 14 Special Teams tackles that season.

Another tackle vs Illinois 2009.

"Football is similar to life in the sense that not every play/day will be easy. There will be times you have to fight and dig deep to make the play and overcome challenges!"

-Donnie Ray Evege-

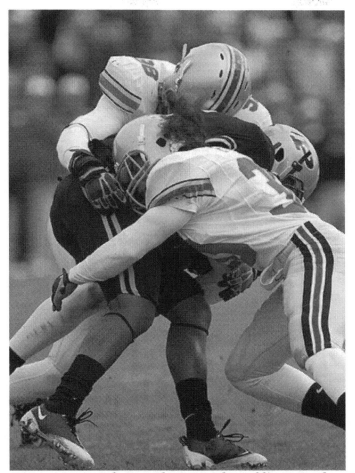

My teammate Solomon Thomas and I tackling a Purdue
Kick Off Returner.

**"Kick Off is similar to *life*. There
will be times on Kick Off where
you can make the *solo* tackle. But
there also be times where you'll
need your teammate next to you
help make "the play." Pursue the**

football as a team, and tackle life's challenges and opportunities off the field as a team as well!"

-Donnie Ray Evege-

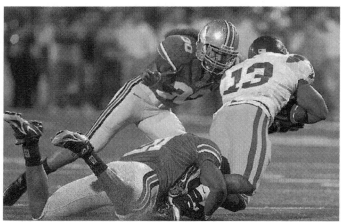

My teammate Anderson Russell and I tackling a USC Kick Off Returner.

My teammate Etienne Sabino and I tackling a New Mexico State Kick Off Returner.

I was an Academic All Big Ten
Conference Student Athlete.

Photo of my Dad, myself, my teammate Michael
Brewster and his dad, Mr. Brewster at our Graduation.
Mike, myself and a lot of my teammates all graduated
with Honors.

Coach Tressel and the entire staff of
counselors at the Younkin Success
Center did a tremendous job at
encouraging their student athletes to
excel in the classroom and in the
Columbus community! The Ohio State
tradition continues to be excel as Coach
Myer and staff motivate and help
prepare the next generation of student

athletes to be champions in all phases of life as well.

On New Years Day, **January 1st, 2010** we were in Pasadena, California to play in what is called, *The Grand Daddy of Them All*, The Rose Bowl!

It was an incredible experience playing in my first Bowl Game, and an exciting game to be a part of!!! It was evenly matched, and a hard fought game.

We ended up taking the lead in the 4th quarter and walking away a victory. The final score was 26 to 17. It felt great to be healthy and *in the game!*

Team celebration after the Rose Bowl Win!

Winter 2010: Coach Tressel and I had a 1 on 1 meeting. Coach Tressel meets with every upper classmen to reflect on the previous season and go over team and individual goals for the following season. My big goal was to be a starter on the defense. Coach Tressel believed in me. He really emphasized how important Spring practice would be for me. I had to take full advantage of the opportunity. I needed to prove more than ever to the coaches that I could *consistently* make plays at Cornerback, and be a valuable asset to the defensive unit.

I left the meeting with Coach Tressel feeling encouraged and ready to earn a Starting position!

Coming into Spring practice I was 2nd string and the number four corner on the depth chart. Due to two corners in front of me getting injured, I moved from the 2nd string number four corner on the depth chart, to now being on the 1st string number two corner on the depth chart. This was the perfect opportunity to show the defensive coaches that I belong on the starting defense!

I felt great and played even better! Throughout Spring ball I had two interceptions returned for touchdowns, several pass deflections, a couple big hits and consistently made solid tackles. I was proving myself and my teammates and media noticed.

Summer 2010: After having an amazing Spring practice, I rode the momentum into summer training and two-a-days. My two teammates who were out of Spring practice got back healthy and regained their spots. I had proven to myself, and a lot people that I was definitely good enough to be a contributor on the starting defense. But, at the end of the day all a player can do is give their best and compete. My focus was to stay prepared and be ready if my name was called. Until then I was going to be the best Special Teams player, and teammate that I could possibly be.

Adversity Strikes (Round 2)

Fall 2010: It was week 3 Ohio U vs OSU at the Shoe. It was a hot, sunny day, over 105,000 people in attendance and millions watching. There was a little more than 10 minutes left in the 2nd quarter when the kick off unit took the field.

We line up. The kicker puts his hand up to signal he's ready to kick. He takes one step...then a second step, and as soon as he takes his third step myself and the other guys all sprint full speed head down during the first phase of our kickoff play.

The football was launched to the 13-yard line.

I see the returner catch it, and start to run to his left. In my peripheral, I see a one teammate get blocked, I see another teammate beat a blocker and I still can see the kickoff returner running.

I see a thin lane to sprint through. I go to make the tackle. I get my hands around his waist, but my angle was slightly off and I missed the tackle.

When I was falling to hit the ground, I instinctively put my hands out to brace my landing. One major problem – the speed at which I landed coupled with my left arm being fully extended during the brace of the fall literally *dislocated* my elbow, tore all of my ligaments, and a tendon.

Photo just seconds after my elbow being dislocated.

I vividly remember hitting the ground, landing face down, staring at the turf, and hearing the play continuing on. During that time, I was in excruciating pain! I felt the pain all over my body.

I heard the whistles and moments after, the trainers were on the ground by my side. They helped me roll over to my right side, and when they saw my elbow sticking out of the socket they immediately threw towels over my arm. They knew the sight was too gruesome for TV and for other people to see.

I was able to stand up and walk to the sideline. I was in so much physical pain, but I was going through even more mental and emotional pain.

With my right hand, I unbuckled my chinstrap, took off my helmet, and threw my helmet against the stadium wall as hard as I could out of frustration, anger and the intensity of that moment. For a brief moment, I honestly felt defeated. The trainers brought the cart to the sideline and drove me to the locker room. While driving down the sideline and through the back end zone, I passed the student section that's underneath the scoreboard. I crossed the student section, cheerleaders, and band. In that moment, the best damn band in the land, the awesome cheerleaders, and the amazing students showed their loving support by wishing me well saying several times, "We love you Donnie!"

Packed with overwhelment from pain, and the loving encouragement from the student section, I put my head down and cried into the towel.

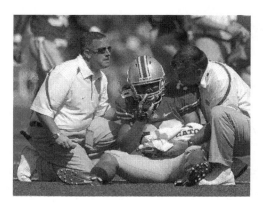

I arrived to the locker room where I'm met with more team trainers and a mobile x-ray machine. They get the results back quickly and determine my arm is not broken, but is dislocated and needed to be popped back in place, immediately.

With 6 hands spread out from my wrist to my shoulder, the doctors and trainers tugged and pushed my elbow back into place. Did it hurt? Yes! The pain was terrible! But not as much as the mental and emotional pain that myself and other athletes, who experience similar situations go through.

I met with the trainers and doctors the next day. I was told it would take the rest of the season to heal, and that I'd possibly be back to practice during Bowl practice. This was yet another major setback. I was sadly beginning to get use to adversity like this.

The doctors warned me that since I had torn all my ligaments and a tendon, there was a possibility that I'd never have full range of motion again.
I felt shock and disbelief at first, but I quickly turned my energy and focus to

regaining full range of motion and getting my arm strong again. *I made the decision at that moment to control what I could control.*

Spring 2011: Thanks to God, extensive rehab and the amazing trainers and student trainers at Ohio State, I regained full range of motion! It took me a little while longer to gain full strength, but that eventually came back as well.

We had recently come off a Sugar Bowl win vs. Arkansas. I had a solid winter conditioning. And I was now ready to compete and give my all to my last Spring football practice as a Buckeye. I was a 5th year senior, and this was it! My last opportunity to fight for a starting position.

Adversity Strikes (Round 3)
I Didn't See That Coming.

It was the first week of practice and we were doing open field tackling drills. I was coming in to strip the football from ball carrier when my teammate came in to make the tackle. As my teammate was bringing the ball carrier to the ground, I instinctively jumped over the pile.

When I landed, I heard what sounded like, *paper tearing*. Unfortunately, that sound, was my ACL.

I had just torn my ACL in my left knee.

I look up and the first person I see is the same person who was there during my first knee injury. Nate Oliver. Nate knew I was in pain and asked, "Are you good?"

First thing I said to him was, "It's a wrap."

I knew that was the last time I'd ever suit up in pads as a Buckeye football player.

DEEP Reflection

It was very difficult to get a taste of what it was like to play on the field, and then not being able to. That's why it's so important to not only play every play like it's your last, but to also cherish every moment you have. Just like your next play in football is not guaranteed, neither is the next day in life.

I suffered three injuries that kept me out the game for a total of 3 plus seasons.

Up to this point, I've given you a timeline of my experiences at Ohio State, and the adversity I faced due to injuries. So much more transpired throughout my time at OSU, but I wanted to show the potential realities you may face as an athlete. Similar adversity can happen at any level, any age and any sport. It's called life. You should always think positive and expect great things to happen. But you must also prepare and plan for "what if."

What if I get injured and have to miss a season? What if I'm not getting as much playing time as I'd like? What if I have a career ending injury and can never play again?

Are you preparing yourself mentally for the possible options that could happen?

I hope you have a safe, healthy and successful sports career! I also hope that after reading my journey as a student athlete, you take your formal education, self education and opportunities more seriously.

The rest of this book is aimed to equip you with mental ammunition that you can use throughout your journey.

Let the chapters that follow empower you to look within so you can release outer greatness.

Keys to Student Athlete Success

Some of the best secrets are hidden *within*.

One great key is that you can get phenomenal results by applying fundamentals on a consistent basis.

When you apply them, it'll feel as though you've found the keys that have unlocked greatness within you. You'll release greater potential that's transferrable to the field!

Study. This one simple word will have a direct *impact* on your career as both a student and as an athlete. The amount of extra time you spend studying outside the classroom will either help you become an Academic All American, or have you stressing out not knowing if you'll receive a passing grade.

Study, in relation to football (or whatever sport you play) will make the difference between you knowing the play your opponent will run prior to the snap, making the big play, winning or losing a game and having the opportunity to play at the next level.

The way you handle pressure is a direct reflection of your preparation.

I created an acronym that I use to remind myself of the importance of what I give my attention to, and how valuable it is to think before I act. I use,

T.I.M.E.

Think Intelligently & Maximize Efficiently.

Think Intelligently with Maximum Effort.

Essentially, this book is a tool. I wrote this book to encourage, educate and empower YOU and student athletes to have a championship mindset, accompanied with stories and techniques that you can use to empower your mind. T.I.M.E is one of those techniques.

My hope is that my writing helps you become the best student athlete you can be during your special journey!

Can you utilize your time better? I think we all can. I strongly encourage you to you use the T.I.M.E. technique throughout your daily life so you can plan more effectively and to mindful to give your best effort. Sports and Life are a journey. It's up to YOU give great effort and enjoy the process.

I've *walked the talk*. I did some things right, and I've done some things wrong. It's my hope that you internalize the *talk I've walked*.

If you learn from my experiences and follow this blueprint for student athlete success, this could be your journey. Whether your journey is similar to mine, or drastically different, you will walk away more equipped to tackle challenges along the way, and you'll have a championship mindset!

It doesn't matter what sport you play or what level you're currently playing, I want this book to empower you and inspire you to be the best athlete and *person* you can be.

Part 2

Ammunition
For
The Athlete

Chapter 4
S.T.O.P

With everything I've experienced, through the success and the setbacks, I've realized that there are always opportunities and options present. Even when I wasn't fully aware, the opportunities were still there.

Two important things to always remember:

1. We always have the gift of choice. We get to choose how we respond to any given situation. You have the option to choose.

2. You have more opportunities present than you realize. All you have to do in order to see opportunities is to make a mental shift. "When you change how you look at things, the things you look at change." This quote is true about your life. Begin viewing your life in a different way. Envision and design your life the way you want it to be.

A mental technique that I created is an acronym for the word, S.T.O.P.

It has several different meanings. Choose whatever meaning works for you in any given situation. Applying the STOP technique will empower your daily life.

STOP

<u>S</u>ee <u>T</u>he <u>O</u>pportunities <u>P</u>resent

Shifting your focus will open new ideas and new doors that once seemed shut.

Seize The **Opportunities** Present

Take full advantage of the opportunities presented to you. There will always be opportunities presented to you. But the same opportunity may not be presented to you twice. Make sure you cherish and respect the blessings that come into your life.

See The Options Present

You always have options. One clear example is that you always have the option to choose how you'll think and respond to a situation.

Choosing your goals, and choosing the people you spend time with and hang around are all options. Always see the options present and choose wisely.

Coach Tressel always impressed upon us players the importance of making the right decision when faced with split second choices. Coach's words have stayed with me for years after playing football for Ohio State. His words are just as true for me now, as when I was still in college.

His advice is also true for you. Every decision comes with either some form of reward or punishment. It's called consequences. **Stay mindful and make sure the decisions that you make today will benefit you tomorrow.**

Throughout your journey you will be faced with temptations and distractions. We live in a fast pace world that is fighting for your attention.

Use this moment right now to take a deep breath. Take several deep breaths if you'd like. Take this moment right now to simply slow down and S.T.O.P.

Make the necassary *shift* in your *perspective* so you can see what's really in front of you.

What opportunities are present in your life?

_____

_____

_____

_____

_____

_____

_____

_____

_____

_____

Worrying won't get you anywhere. Second-guessing won't get you anywhere either. **When you take control of your mind, you then begin to take control of your life.**

When you enhance your mental awareness by using the mental technique S.T.O.P., you will literally begin to *transform your life*. I'm talking about your entire life circumstances. This is simple. But "simple" is not always easy.

Can you do this? Yes!

But it's not what I think that's important.

*It's what you **believe** that's important.*

Make the *shift*.

Change your mindset and enhance your attitude through stopping and being aware.

Don't use your past as an excuse. **Use what you've been through as ammunition to push forward even further.** You've made it through, and you're continuing to make it through. Excuses kill greatness. You were born to be great! Live courageously with confidence.

Always remember: You first have to *see* it in your mind. Then you have to *seize* it in your life. Opportunities will always be there, but the same opportunities may not always present themselves twice.

Maximize it!

I think we can all agree that tomorrow is not promised to anyone.

Life is a gift.

The time for YOU is now. Seize every opportunity presented to you!

The opportunity would not be placed in front of you if you didn't have it *within* you to achieve it.

What are you waiting for? Do things today that your future self will thank you for.

The **TIME** is Now.
It's your time to

Think Intelligently,
Maximize Efficiently

DEEP Questions

1. What opportunities are present to you that you may have been overlooking?

2. What are your options?

3. What are your aspirations?

4. What are the steps that you need to take in order for you to achieve them?

5. How can you utilize your T.I.M.E. better? How can you *think more intelligently while maximizing more efficiently* in your life?

Chapter 5
The Inside Game

❖ Master Your Mind, Master Your Game, Master Your Life

- *Athletic Ability Is Not Enough*

It takes so much more than just athletic ability in order to be successful. It takes the intangibles, which I'll talk about here really soon. It takes time management skills. It takes confidence. It takes courage. It takes humility. You never know everything and you have to strive to constantly be a student and a learner. There will be times where you'll have the opportunity to be in the position to teach someone else. You'll be the mentor, but you will always be a mentee to someone else. The greats all know this. They're constantly studying. They're constantly learning from the people that came before them. They're constantly studying and evaluating film. In short, they're never satisfied. They stay hungry. They have a certain kind of confidence and they always demonstrate humility. *Stay Hungry. Stay Humble.*

- The Intangibles

Control what you can control. Only God can control if you're going to be 6'5" or if you're going to be 5'4". That's tangible. But what can you control?

You can always control the Intangibles. I've put together 5 Intangibles that we all individually can control. They are:
1. Mindset
2. Attitude
3. Effort
4. Decision making / Priorities
5. Sacrifices

Your Mindset – This is the big picture. What are you thinking about? What's your perspective on life? And what's your perspective on your current circumstances? Are you living to your full potential? If you need some fine-tuning, I highly encourage you to tune up and turn up your mindset. A truth in life is, **what you think about, you bring about.**

Attitude – When I say attitude I'm really talking about your *daily* attitude. When you enter practice with a great attitude, practice goes great. On the flip side, if you enter practice with a poor attitude it's extremely hard to get your energy up and give a championship level effort. Always remember; **your energy is contagious.** Be on purpose when choosing your daily attitude.

Effort – Intangible #3 could very easily be ranked #1. Only you can determine how much effort or lack thereof you give. When you want to be,
*the best version of yourself,
*the best athlete
*the best student
*and the best well-rounded person...you'll make the conscious decision to give your best at everything you do. Always remember, every small detail matters. **Give your best no matter how big or small the task is**. And always go the extra mile and do more than what is expected. Over deliver with results. You can over deliver on your results by caring about what you do and giving your best effort every play, and on every classroom assignment.

Decision making – Your decisions today affect your tomorrows. Everything has a consequence. *Everything.* It's up to you if that consequence is a punishment or a reward. Choose wisely what you give your attention to. Choose wisely who you hang with. An old saying, "You are the accumulation of the 5 people you spend time with the most." Another one is "Show me your friends, I'll show you your future." Make sure your inner circle consists of people that encourage you and that lift you up. And make sure you are that to other people. Our future is greatly influenced by the decisions we make today.

Priorities – First things first. Don't make the mistake of putting third things first. What's most important? What are your top daily priorities? These are things to ask yourself and that need answered. Whatever you decide is top priority; make it your mission to follow your agenda.

Sacrifices – What should you give up? Better asked, what do you *need* to give up in order for you to move forward? What are you willing to give up to be great? What's holding you back from reaching your goals? For some of us, we may need to give up our phones and social media for a certain time period so we can focus and lock in on our priorities. **Effective time management is critically important**. Some of us need to give up our fears. Is fear holding you back? If so, why? Keep reading. If you shift your perspective and use the techniques in this book, I'm confident that you will have better results. Some of us also need to stretch ourselves and get out of our comfort zones. **A limited mind will get limited results.** Think bigger. Think bolder. YOU have untapped potential and I want to help you release it!

After reading this chapter, I want you to move on knowing that you have control over your life. You have the opportunity to control your intangibles. *Believe* me when I say that the intangibles will have tangible results. The intangibles are all within your grasp. Like I always say, "Go deep within to bring outer excellence."

To go deep within means you're taking control of the Intangibles.

Athletic Alchemy is transforming your inner world to enhance your outer experiences.

Ways to do that are to control what you can control, to realize the potential you have, to grasp the opportunities you have, and to take action.

Chapter 6
IDENTITY

❖ Know Your Number

In high school, I wore #5 and #32. In college my jersey was 30, but my true number was always #1. You may be a high school student athlete reading this book right now or you may be a professional athlete.

I don't care what your number on your jersey is from 0 to 99. In your heart you need to realize and remember that your true identity and your true number is Number One. Knowing your true number means you have a better grasp on your identity. **You make the jersey number. The jersey number does not make you.** You have to train and perform and think as if you are the star player. Nobody wants to go to battle on game day with a player who second guesses themselves, who questions their own abilities or who feels like they're not good enough. To make the biggest impact on your team and in your personal career, you have to *feel* as though you are the *Star Player*. And your work has to back that.

In the Athletic Alchemy concept, being the Star Player does not mean you know it all. It does not mean you are a pre-madonna. It does not mean that you're selfish and don't care about your teammates and team. The true meaning of being a Star Player, within this context, means that you are *unselfish*. It means that you are a leader. It means that you are an extremely diligent and hard worker. It means that you are intelligent and a student of the game.

Being a Star Player means you've earned everything you've received. Being the Star Player means that you realize the position you are in and you realize and value the leadership role that you have. Being the Star Player that you are, you realize the responsibility that you have to yourself, to your teammates, to your coaches and to your community. Be a Star Player and surround yourself with other Star Players.

❖ Know Who You Are and Whose You Are

In sports and in life, it is so important to know who you are. Even better said, it is so important to know *who you are* and *whose you are*. I'm going to take a moment to empower your mind with encouraging words and true statements:

- You are a limitless being.
- You have so much untapped potential just waiting to be released to the world.
- You were created for greatness. When you tap within and fully realize who you are, I guarantee you that you will get better results.
- You are part of this magical universe and you were created by the Most High.
- God has a purpose for you and is by your side.
- Walk with confidence.
- Train with confidence.
- Perform with confidence.
- Think with confidence. Everything you do, do it with confidence.

- Visualize and goal set knowing that what your mind can conceive you can attract into your reality.
- Take time every day for personal development.
- Take time every day to develop your inner world so that your outer experiences are amazing.

When you know WHO YOU Are and WHOSE YOU Are, you are now walking into a new world, a new perception where your dreams can come true and you literally become the best YOU possible.

❖ *Athletic Depression*

You're used to being "The Man" your entire life. Then you get to college and there's a full team of players that were "The Man" too. The competition standards have risen drastically. Every play seems to be evaluated by your coaches more in depth compared to when you played at the previous level.

There will be times when things don't go the way you want. For the first time in your life, you may not be first string on the depth chart. That can potentially be a blow to your ego and to your confidence.... (only if you let it). So, with that being said, there's a recipe for a potential athletic depression. It doesn't just happen when you're competing. It also happens when your athletic career is over.

Depression can come from so much pressure from family, friends, community/your hometown, and self-imposed pressure. The most intense pressure is *self-imposed*. That equates to weight. Have you ever felt the weight of the world on your shoulders? When you have pressure in your life, good pressure or bad pressure or both, it's invisible but you can feel it. Let go. Let God. Let go of all unnecessary weight. Here's something that I want you to know. You don't have to carry that extra weight. You have a choice. You can make the conscious decision to focus on what's most important. **What's important is being at your best. You're at your best when you're not overthinking.** You're at your best when instincts take over and your quality preparation allows for your athleticism to shine. Pressure, which will equal weight, will weigh you down and negatively impact your performance. Yes, you need goals. Yes, you need to have standards. Yes, there is such a thing as having high expectations that can feel like a form of pressure, but take what I'm saying as getting rid of all unnecessary mental weight.

When an athlete suffers an injury, there is no doubt that he or she will experience some form of depression during their journey of initial injury, through the lengthy stages of rehab.

❖ I Am More Than My Jersey

There's more to you than just football or whatever sport you play. To the corporate executive reading this, you are more than just your title. Sometimes we fall into the trap of thinking we are only our profession. **Always remember that you are so much more than your "title" and jersey number.**

❖ Mentality Shapes Reality

Mentality shapes reality. What you think about, you bring about. The law of attraction is very real. As athletes, visualization is a major key to success. The power of the athlete's mind is limitless. It's your job as an athlete to train your mind. It's your job to cultivate and create a perspective that positions you for the best success. What do you want your reality to be? Your mentality is the key. Do you want to be a starter? Do you want a promotion? Do you want certain changes to happen in your life? Begin within. Start with intangible #1 Mindset. Your mentality and outlook on life is the biggest difference maker.

❖ Show Me Your I.D.

If I asked you to show me your I.D. and you decided to do so, what would you show me? Your driver's license or some other photo with your name attached to it? A picture showing your brown or blue eyes, long or short hair, smile or frown. That would be my initial thought. But in this case when I ask to see your I.D. I'm not talking about anything related to your photo, name or data on a card. In this case I'm referring to your **"Inner Dialogue."**

What does your I.D. look like in this case? Our lives have a major correlation between where we are and how we talk to ourselves. Inner dialogue has a profound impact on our lives!

The KEY Is Your I.D

You hold the key. You can unlock any door that has appeared to be locked. That "key" is your "I.D."

Are you your biggest supporter? Are you giving yourself constant encouragement and positive reinforcement in your mind? Or, are you having lots of negative self talks and thoughts with yourself? Are you letting fear and self-doubt limit you and hold you back from taking action in your daily life?

Your inner dialogue plays a critical part in whether you achieve your dreams (or even pursue your dreams). Your positive inner dialogue can play a major role with helping you achieve your goals and shape your destiny. Belief & Faith can take you to unimaginable heights.... and having a negative I.D. can take you to a very low place. You have the power. You have the choice. Choose a deeper more encouraging dialogue within yourself and watch the miracles that take place.

I want to encourage you and show you ways to better enhance your Inner Dialogue so you are more positive and optimistic.

❖ **Create A New I.D.**

Use the following affirmations as a tool to raise your vibration and jump start your conscious brain:

1 "I Am....." For example: Say you're currently in a second string position, but you aspire to be a first string starter. Your affirmation would read as, "I am a starter." Another example, let's say you're an athlete who's running the 40 yard dash in 4.6 seconds, but your goal is to run the 40 yard dash in 4.4 seconds. Your affirmation would be "I am a 4.4 40 yard dash athlete."

2 "I have...."

3 "I feel love and abundance in my life. I am attracting the best people to help me achieve my dreams."

4 "I know God watches over me and my loved ones, and that God has a plan for me." I know this because I have a plan for myself. God resides within me.

It's up to you to customize your affirmations in accordance to your ultimate end goal. When you use these affirmations, you are putting yourself into position to have greater results. Take charge. Begin right now in creating and developing a new I.D. Use present tense. Do this multiple times a day. Don't let fear hold you back and limit the amount of success and happiness you have in your life.

Take the message, and *leave* the delivery.

A quick piece of advice on how to receive feedback from authority figures.

There will be times in your life when someone says something in a *tone* you don't like. It could be a parent, teacher, coach or boss.

You will become a better player and person once you learn to *take the message* they are sending you, and *leave the delivery.*

People aren't perfect. People will talk to you in a way that you won't agree with. For example, some coaches yell and scream to get their points across. That's great if you're a player who likes *that style* of communication. But if you don't like yelling and screaming, you have to S.T.O.P, get past the noise and find the true message they are attempting to convey.

Once you can take the message, apply the message and be coachable, you'll become a more mature, and well rounded athlete.

Chapter 7
Tackling Tears

❖ **Overwhelming Obstacles**

It was a beautiful sunny day in
Columbus, Ohio and I was walking
through the Oval after leaving a
geography class. It was my first spring at
OSU, and at the time I was taking 18
credits and participating in Spring
Football. Needless to say, I had a lot on
my plate. I had a few extra minutes
between classes, so I decided to sit down
for a moment and take a breather. I
spotted a huge shade tree and sat down
in the shade. All of a sudden I started
crying and I just couldn't control it. I
wasn't bawling, but I just couldn't stop
the tears from coming. I then decided to
pick up the phone and call that one
person I knew would answer... my mom.
I said, "Mom, I want to come home."
And she did what any good mother
would do in that situation. She listened.
I said, "I just want to be a regular guy. I
want to go to a local school back home
and just be regular." My experience up
until that point was overwhelming. She
gave me the best advice at that moment.
She replied, "Ray, I know you're going

through a lot, and I know you're overwhelmed, but if you stay you'll be happy you did." She encouraged me to stay. I'm glad she did!

I didn't know it at the time, but what I was experiencing was common. After talking to other student athletes, I learned very quickly that almost all of them had times where they felt extreme pressure, overwhelment and stress. In my heart, I did not want to quit. I had worked my entire life to be in the position I was in. It was an honor and a blessing. To whom much is given, much is expected. I had to make a shift. A mental shift. I had to put all my focus on why I was there and what my purpose was.

DEEP Reflection

During those *trying* times, there were moments I was not at my best. There were times where I made poor decisions that did not add any value to my life. No one is perfect. **The thing to always remember is that when we make poor decisions or make a mistake, we must *learn* from those experiences.** When we learn and apply what we learn, that is wisdom. To take it a step further, in my opinion, when we learn from other peoples' mistakes and success, that is a truer, deeper level of wisdom. Be observant. Be a student. Be a lifelong learner.

Even in your own adversity, you can still be an encouragement to someone else. You're still an athlete. You're still part of the team. You still have that fellowship with other athletes. Your role may change while you're injured, but it's an opportunity for you to come back even stronger mentally. You may not realize that while you're going through it, but I'm writing this to tell you that if you persevere you have the opportunity to come back a stronger, more well-rounded person. This is where your testimony can become your treasure.

Tremendous Adversity:
A Tribute To My Teammate

Dan Potakar*: Wide Receiver #83*
Grove City, Ohio.

Who would have known that my very
first tackle as an Ohio State Buckeye
would be against my teammate, Dan
Potakar, in the 2007 Scarlet vs Grey
Spring game? We would have never
guessed that shortly after that he would
be tackling cancer. Even in that
tremendous adversity, Dan remained
involved and was a key member of our
team. I vividly remember a hot summer
day in early August right before camp
began. Every year we would have our
conditioning test the week before 2-a-
days started. The conditioning test is
extremely challenging even for the guys
who are in great shape. The year before I
had failed the test. Due to failing the
test, I had to wake up every morning
during the first week of camp at 5am
and do an aquatic workout. Myself and
the other guys who didn't pass the
conditioning test would catch the bus
around 5:15am outside of our hotel and
go straight to the R-Pack building. The
strength coaches would put us through a

rigorous training session under water. And by the time the workout was over we were physically drained. So, to say the very least, there is a lot riding on passing the conditioning test! No one wants to have to lose 2 hours of sleep and do an extra workout during the 3 weeks of 2-a-days where football is at its most grueling.

Dan Potakar is extremely selfless and cares about his team. During a time where he was battling cancer, he still showed up to to be there for his teammate's morale and to be encouraging.

The gasser test consisted of going down and back the width of the field, 53 ½ yards down and 53 1/2 yards back. Each player had to do that 20 times. Depending on your position a player had to finish in a set amount of time. For the skilled players (Wide Receivers and Defensive Backs) the first 10 down and backs, had to finish the sprint in 16 seconds with a 30 second break in between sets. The last 10 down and backs, each player gets an additional second to make their time with a 45 second rest. Some guys like Brian

Heartline, Malcome Jenkins, Kurt
Coleman, Dane Sazenbacher, Cameron
Heyward, and Brian Rolle passed the
gasser test every time. But, for me, I
struggled. Once I would get to sprint #9,
my lower back and legs would start to
get tight. Around #14 it gets harder to
catch your breath. The gasser test is set
up to not only test your physical
condition, but it's also designed to test
your mental condition. This is where
Dan Potakar helped me.

Dan took it upon himself to stay by my
side and wait right there at the starting
point every sprint for me. Where I
struggled the previous year during the
test I still struggled that day, but I had
Dan there to give me support and
encouragement, "Come on Donnie, YOU
GOT THIS!", "Keep going!", "You're
doing great, let's go!". Seeing and having
Dan there gave me a mental *edge*.
Where Dan came in clutch was after
every sprint when I crossed the finish
line he'd be right there with that green
Gatorade bottle filled with ice cold
water. I'm leaned over exhausted in that
August humidity in the Shoe and here's
Dan right there ready and willing to help
me pass each and every sprint.... all 20

of them. He kept me and other guys hydrated. When my lower back started to get tight and when it was getting harder for me to breathe, he would spray the cold water on my neck and back which gave temporary relief and helped to expand my lungs so I could breathe in more air. I could say, *I* passed the conditioning test, but that would only be partly true. *We*, Dan and I, passed the test together.

What Dan demonstrated throughout his career at Ohio State, and especially that day for me, was what being a team player is all about. Dan didn't have to be there that morning. He had bigger battles than passing a conditioning test, but he made the conscious decision to not only be there, but also be directly involved and hands on in helping his teammates. No one would have blamed Dan for not being there. No one would have blamed Dan for focusing his attitude and energy solely on himself. Seeing Dan not only battle and fight cancer, but to also see Dan in the team meetings, at practices, and around the facility, made me realize even more that battling adversity is a daily fight.

You may have to stare it right in the face, but just know that when adversity strikes, and it will strike, that you have the choice to strike back, overcome, win, and become an even stronger person through it all.

A Tribute To My Teammate

Tyson Gentry: Special Teams & Wide Receiver #24 *Sandusky, Ohio.*

I had the privilege of spending time with Tyson during the 2007-2008 season. Tyson's story is beyond inspirational. He demonstrates the epitome of having an "attitude of gratitude." I'm going to write directly from his Foundation's website at www.newperspectivefoundation.org

"Tyson is originally from Sandusky, Ohio and is the youngest of three kids born to Bob and Gloria. He graduated from Perkins High School in 2004 and went to The Ohio State University to earn his degree in Speech and Hearing Science. Tyson chose Ohio State because he grew up as a Buckeye fan and was recruited as a preferred walk-on for the

football team. He was recruited as a punter but also played wide receiver in high school, so he eventually started contributing as a scout team receiver as well.

Going into the spring of Tyson's sophomore year, he was asked to focus exclusively on playing receiver. On April 14, 2006, Tyson's life changed in a split second. **During a routine play in a team scrimmage, he hit the ground awkwardly while being tackled and was instantly paralyzed from the neck down.** *Over the next week, he had two surgeries to stabilize his neck with titanium rods and cadaver bone. Prayers started immediately from family, friends, and strangers who had heard Tyson's story in the news. After that, it was a waiting game to see how much the swelling and trauma to his spinal cord would effect his mobility and sensation.*

Tyson started inpatient therapy after two weeks in the ICU and step-down unit. He worked with an occupational and physical therapist for about three months before leaving the hospital and starting outpatient therapy. He eventually regained movement in his biceps and also has reduced sensation throughout his body. Tyson considers himself extremely blessed to have regained the movement and sensation he has today. Having the perspective of knowing what it was like to rely on someone for everything has really helped him appreciate life much more than he ever did. Tyson may not be able to do half of what he could before his injury, but he can still do a lot with what he still has."

I was a recruit watching Ohio State's practice the day Tyson was severely injured. I witnessed the play that changed people's lives forever. I also witnessed part of the journey that has inspired and uplifted people's lives forever!

Tyson has a way of engaging people and encouraging them to stay positive no matter what is going on in life. I remember Tyson and I sitting poolside during down time at the 2008 National Championship in New Orleans. It was a gorgeous day outside, and a lot of our football family were relaxing and enjoying the short break time we had away from practice and film study.

During our talk, Tyson asked me how I was dealing with my knee injury and if there was anything that he could do for me. We talked about life, purpose and how blessed we all truly are.

Tyson demonstrates positive ways to overcome adversity and have a mindset of service. Tyson and his wife Megan have created the New Perspective Foundation whose mission is to serve the community by providing financial assistance, motivational speaking, and other contributions to individuals living with disabilities or dealing with medical issues especially people and families who have experienced spinal cord injuries.

Tyson, his wife Megan, his parents Bob and Gloria and their entire family are blessings to the world and continue to demonstrates God's love through their actions and philanthropic work.

Have a Healthy Game Plan

There is a friend of my family whose name is Dave Wilson. Dave is the stepfather of NFL ProBowler, Trent Cole. Trent is 6 years older than me. Our families went to church together.

Once I committed to play football at Ohio State, Dave gave my dad a valuable piece of advice that we all can learn from. He said, "Donnie Ray is going to have to find healthy outlets to relieve stress."

Trent is an outdoors man. Some of his passions and healthy outlets are fishing and hunting. He played college football at the University of Cincinnati. After his games, while other guys would party, Trent would be en route to hunt in the woods. Trent's passions and healthy outlets like hunting and fishing may not be mine or your healthy outlets, but the takeaway of the story is that Mr. Dave Wilson is spot on. We all must have healthy outlets throughout our entire life. Not just after a football game, not just after a stressful day at work, but all the time.

What are your healthy outlets? Some healthy outlets that I personally like are reading a fascinating, nonfiction book. I thoroughly enjoy journaling and documenting my life through video diaries (for my family to have once I'm gone). I enjoy weight training. I enjoy the simple things like spending quality time with family and friends. Whatever your healthy outlets are, I encourage you to use them and not resort to negative outlets which only result in *self-destructive* behaviors. Choose the better path. Your future self will thank you.

- Negative Ways of Coping

Negative ways of coping are using drugs, alcohol, and reckless behavior to somehow try and fill a void.

Don't bottle your emotions only to release them through a bottle. It's a temporary fix for lasting pain. The solution is to honor your emotions in a healthy way. Talk to a trusted friend or professional and think long term.

If you've been using unhealthy outlets, you can change now. There's no better time than right now, this moment.

You're the author of your life. You hold the pen. If you don't like your past behaviors or the results you've been getting, I have great news for you.

Your next chapter is completely blank, and you have control to fill it with greatness!

Don't bottle up your emotions only to release them through a bottle.

- Healthy Ways of Overcoming

Coping is not overcoming. It's a bandage for a bigger problem. Coping is a part of the process, but it's not the final step.

Throughout your athletic career and throughout your life journey, there will be distractions that present themselves.

These distractions come in different shapes, forms, and sizes. When distractions and temptations come your way, one of the most important things to do in that moment is to remember **why** you do what you do. You have to have more *will* and fortitude and be bigger than whatever distraction comes your way. Be bigger and stronger than negativity that comes your way. Own it. Overcome it.

Talk to a professional. Some of the most elite athletes have professional counselors and therapists that they talk to often. Instead of holding on to the stigma that some people have of a negative connation when someone talks to a professional, change your perception. By talking to a professional, your game and life will be enhanced. You will have greater clarity. You will achieve better results in all areas of your life. Use your resources. For many of you who are collegiate athletes, you have professional psychologists that are right there on campus able to help you upon your request.

Positive Ways to Cope
- Journal
- Read personal development books
- Listen to empowering podcasts
- Spend time with your support system i.e. friends that uplift and encourage you, family who have your best interest at heart
- Exercise
- Anything productive. *Be productive versus self-destructive.* Ask yourself, "is what I'm about to do productive or self-destructive?"

You are equipped. In your heart, you know what's productive. You know the way. Make the play by every day, every decision, choosing productive behaviors rather than destructive behaviors. When you decide to choose yourself, the process will be more fulfilling and you'll enjoy the journey.

❖ My Mom Was Right

When I called her Spring of 2007 crying under a tree, feeling overwhelmed, and having a moment of "wanting to go home", she was right with the advice she gave me. Again, I never wanted to go home. Just in the moment as an early enrollee, everything was new and extremely challenging.

I am a better and stronger person for having persevered through all the challenges that I faced as being a student athlete and football player at Ohio State. It was not easy, but it was rewarding. I have so much gratitude towards my support system of family, friends, teammates, and the behind the scenes staff at the university.

It truly does take a team of people for an individual to achieve success. And just like my mom was right with the advice she gave me, her advice would be true if given to you. Stay. Finish.

Your Story Is Your Treasure.

Right now, this very moment, you can rewrite the direction of where your life story goes. Go up. Go forward. Go with courage. Go with faith.

You don't know what you don't know. What lies ahead could be a lot better than your current or past situation. The takeaway is, *keep going*. You haven't lived tomorrow yet. Live in the present. Don't time travel in the past.

DEEP Reflection

The key takeaway here is having a great support system, making the shift by changing your outlook on things, and taking necessary steps along the way of your journey to allow the best outcomes possible. (In this case, I adjusted my schedule and reduced my class load while still remaining a full time student.)

You don't know what you don't know. What lies ahead could be a lot better than your current or past situation.

Part 3

Striving To Be More

Chapter 8
You Are One Degree Away From Achieving Your Dream

Always bring your A game. You never know who someone else knows. Position yourself for success. Make yourself available to receive blessings by putting yourself in position where your talents can shine and you can help others.

Know the down and distance.
One of the first things a football player needs to know in the beginning of a new play is the down and distance. Is it third down and seven yards to go? Or is it fourth down and one yard to go? Depending on what down it is and how close the offense is to the first down marker will determine the play call. How does this relate to life? Some of you are so close to getting a first down on the next play, but you may be tired, you may feel overwhelmed, and you may be afraid. And because of that, you may quit when you are so close to having a successful next play. In football you want to keep the first down chains moving. When you continue to get first

downs you'll eventually score a touchdown.

If you persevere and don't quit in life, in whatever you're going through, your next play could not only be a first down, it could be a game/life changing play that results in a game winning touchdown.

Don't let fear hold you back. Give all your attention and focus on the play at hand.

So, where are you in your current circumstance?

Are you just starting off a new project, a new venture or a new goal?

If so, it would be 1st and 10 with the ball on your 20 yard line. You're in the beginning stages. Put more sweat equity in. *Ramp up your ambition* but also have patience.

Are you on the goal line? In your life, is it 4th and goal? In which case, PUSH. Go harder. Dig deep and give everything you have to score!

Chapter 9
Someone Is Always Watching You

❖ My 8ᵗʰ Grade Year

My 8ᵗʰ grade year was one of the most impactful years of my life. One of the reasons is because of who I became, and the lessons I learned. I always knew that having a strong work ethic along with dedication would eventually pay off, but this year in particular made it extremely evident.

While after school, most kids used their time to play video games and do other things, but Ryan, Bryan and I had a vision. Part of that vision entailed us transforming our bodies and minds in preparation for high school football. The by-product was not only the physical transformation of our bodies, we also had the opportunity to develop relationships with the upperclassmen and the coaching staff.

Every day immediately after school we would hustle to the bus that drove kids to the high school. We'd get off the bus and went directly to the weight room.

There were times when the workouts for the high school players would be mandatory and sometimes they were voluntary. For 8th graders like us, we were invited to

We were determined to be exceptional.

participate but our attendance was not mandatory. *We didn't care if it was mandatory or optional. We were determined to be exceptional.*

We trained with the varsity football team every day. It wasn't long before we saw tangible results. We got stronger (the numbers in our lifts went up), our bodies began to develop and transform into better-conditioned athletes, and our speed and agility numbers saw constant improvement. We started gaining the respect of not only our future teammates, we also gained the attention and respect of then Head Football Coach, Coach Paul Jenne, and staff.

I remember another 8th grader happened to come to the high school workout. After the workout, I decided to do more and changed into a sleeveless shirt. I started curling dumbbells and this newbie was surprised at how much weight I was lifting and how my muscles developed. The kid said in a serious tone, "Donnie, it looks like you've been on steroids." He didn't ask a question, but I could tell he wanted a response. Coach Jenne was nearby and overheard this kid's comment. Coach Jenne proudly said, "Donnie's been on that *iron!*" I always felt that hard work would get noticed, and at that moment I knew that Coach Jenne recognized the hard work that I had been putting in. Man, did that feel good.

❖ The Janitor Who Impacted My Life

When I was in the 8th grade I met a janitor at school, his name was Norm Nelson. A lot of times kids don't show as much respect to janitors as they should.

Mr. Nelson pulled me to the side one day and said, "Donnie, I've been watching you. You're having success with your middle school football team. You're doing great, but I'm more impressed with how you carry yourself and how you treat people. I want you to know that I'm not just a janitor. I'm also an Official for the Big 10 Football Conference!"

He went on to educate me on what high school and college coaches look for in a student athlete, and what I should expect at the next level. He told me that coaches at the college level want guys with good character who take their academics seriously, who attack every play with high intensity and guys who are true leaders among their peers.

That's just a quick story on you never know who is watching you. If you say something, have a purpose with it because there are always ears listening and eyes watching.

DEEP Reflection

Everything you do needs to be intentional and have a purpose.

❖ **Showing Up**

Half the battle is won by simply showing up! Dedication with a persistent mindset will give you optimal opportunities for success.

❖ **Timing**

The right people, circumstances and events will enter your life in order for your vision to *manifest*.

Chapter 10
Remember What You Represent

It's critically important that you remember that YOU Are a BRAND. You represent not only yourself as a personal brand, but also the organization that you're a part of. Why is knowing that important? Everything you do is being watched. Everything you do is critiqued. Every move you make is being evaluated. This goes for how you carry yourself in person, at public events, and on social media. You're a brand and your team is a brand. And *you are a reflection of your team.*

Companies are looking for and giving people sponsorship deals based on the reputation that a person has created. This could be big time endorsement deals from Fortune 500 companies. Wouldn't it be nice if you had an opportunity to partner with a company that you believed in and that believed in you? Well, you can. You don't have to be the biggest name out there like Tiger Woods, Michael Jordan, or Lebron James to get a deal. There are deals being made at every level, every day. Be on purpose, develop your own brand, and be consistent. Give yourself an opportunity to be discovered by positioning yourself to be viewed as a person who adds value. Always bring your A game.

{ Always remember;

YOU Are A BRAND. }

Chapter 11
Tackling Temptations

What you want to be and who you want to become has to be greater than the temptation that you're facing in your current situation.

Know Yourself

You know yourself better than anybody else does. Know your pitfalls. Have a plan of attack. Know what tempts you. Know what can sabotage your success *before* you get confronted. What happens if you fall into temptation? What then? If and when you fall into temptation, whether we call it a mistake or just a setback, learn from that experience. Try your absolute best not to fall in that same manner again. Time waits for no one. You literally do not have time to make the same mistakes over and over again. You have to learn from your past mistakes. When you make mistakes over and over again, you waste time. You can maximize your time most effectively when you execute your plan.

When I was an Ohio State football

player, Coach Tressel would constantly emphasize how critical it was for us as young men to make the right decisions. The seniors and the coaching staff knew that we were under a microscope. Every major college program is. For that reason, every decision we made would get magnified in the public eye. **Coach Tressel would say that a 3 second decision could affect the rest of your life.** Coach Tressel's words are true. They remain true for myself. And they are true for you.

How have your past decisions impacted your life today? Also, ask yourself what can I do differently moving forward, to make my life better than my past? Use the S.T.O.P. technique that we talked about earlier in the book, and keep Coach Tressel's words of wisdom in the forefront of your mind. Every decision matters. Every decision counts.

The Decisions You Make Today Will Impact You Tomorrow!

Chapter 12
Don't Fall Into The Traps Of Self-Sabotage

Your mind can either be your greatest asset or enemy. The empowering news is you get to choose. This means you get to design your life. Give yourself a fighting chance to win at whatever you pursue. The game is played in your mind *first*. That goes for any game, whether it be football, school, work, or anything. The game is won or lost in the mind.

{ **Excuses kill Greatness!** }

A few things that high achievers and successful people have in common are that they take responsibility, accountability, and they do not make excuses. Champions realize that there is no room for excuses. Not everything will go their way. Not everything will go smoothly. There are plenty of times where unfortunate situations on the field and in life are not their fault. The important thing to internalize here is the attitude and intent of being a person that doesn't make excuses. It's not about the words. It's about the mindset. Successful people don't think about excuses. They're busy grinding and moving forward.

Next play. Unfortunate things are going to happen to you. At some point in your career you will experience a bad play in your sport. You may drop the ball. You may miss a tackle. You may throw an interception. Own your actions. Take responsibility for your results. The key here is *next play*. Next play is a mental technique. Just like you're likely to have bad plays, you will also experience amazing plays. Plays where you make a great tackle, score the winning touchdown, or make the key block that positions your teammate for the first down or touchdown. Have the mental maturity to move on. Move on no matter what. Yesterday is gone. You can't get it back. The previous play is over. You can't play it again. But what you can do is focus on the next play. If you want the next play to be your *best play*, you have to be present. What's your role right now? Staying focused can be difficult at times, but laser back in and ask yourself, "What is my role right now for this day and this play?" What should I do to position myself to allow me to become the person I need to be? Only you can figure that out.

Ways of falling into the traps of self-sabotage include
- Overthinking
- Questioning your worth
- Spending too much time questioning things you cannot control
- Making excuses
- Lacking accountability
- Not taking personal responsibility
- Self-doubt
- Negative self-talk
- Being influenced by destructive peer pressure
- Not having a purpose bigger than yourself
- Not having a *why* that's bigger than just you

Ways to avoid self-sabotage include
- Spend time often with people that remind you of your greatness. "But

what if I don't have people like
that in my life?" Be that for
somebody else. Initiate and ignite
somebody else's greatness, and in
return it's likely they'll do the
same for you. You be the change.

Remember to do the following things:
- Build your tribe.
- Remember to use the S.T.O.P
technique.
- Remember your ideal I.D.
- DEEP affirmations
- Self-care
- Self-love

You can prevent self-sabotage by
remembering your greatness, by
remembering and being mindful of all
that you're capable of, and being
mindful that you are a limitless being.
Believe in yourself. All self-sabotage is,
is having a hiccup in your mindfulness.

Chapter 13
Awaken Your Network Within – Keeping Faith

*All things are possible
to those who believe.*

Your traditional network is the people that directly affect your life and the people you spend the most time with. Your network *within* is that quiet, still place where the invisible becomes visible. *Within is where the manifestation process transcends.* So, how can you utilize this? You utilize this by tapping in and asking. Know what you want, meditate, visualize, and take action towards what you want. The universe rewards those who know what they want, who ask, and who take action.

God is your greatest resource. There's nothing you can't do when you're tuned in to the highest power. There's so much that you can achieve and become when you're tapped in. Cherish this moment. Realize that time is valuable. Develop a deeper relationship with God. Once you do this, your life will begin to change.

Awaken your network with these keys
- Know what you want
- Be true to yourself
- Meditate
- Visualize
- Create a vision board
- Believe you are capable
- Know you have value
- Have courage and confidence
- Utilize your imagination and dream BIG.
- Go for it!

DEEP Reflections

Know that God has blessed you with unique gifts, and that you have untapped potential that's just waiting to be released to the world! The world needs what you have to offer.

Chapter 14
Be A Leader And
Follow Other Leaders

How do you become a leader? There are
many different components on the topic
of leadership. Part of becoming a leader
is having a willingness to,

- Learn
- Being able to not let others'
  opinions outweigh what's right
- Take action and execute
  consistently
- Study leaders because success
  leaves clues.
- Lead by example.
- Be a lifelong student. There's
  always more to learn.
- Build a support system.
- Associate and spend time with
  like-minded people who are goal-
  oriented.
- Get mentored.
- Be a mentor. Pass on your
  knowledge and be the person to
  someone else that you want in
  your life.

And remember, every leader was once a
beginner.

> *"A journey of a thousand miles*
> *begins with the first step"*
> *- Lao Tzu*

Take the first step to becoming the best
You that you can become.

Chapter 15
How To Become The Greatest Version Of Yourself

You become the greatest version of yourself by putting to use the following

- Set goals.
- Be intentional.
- Discipline yourself.
- Push yourself to achieve greatness.
- Read, watch, and listen to material that will uplift your spirit.
- Always seek to improve yourself.
- Practice your craft.
- Invest in yourself.
- Know your worth.
- Know that you are worthy.

A major part of becoming the greatest version of yourself is simply wanting to. When you want to, then you become deliberate. When you become deliberate that brings purposeful action. Once you're taking action, you're fully entering your self-empowerment.

Be the best version of yourself possible. Along the journey of being your best self, keep the 3 C's in mind.

1. Choices
2. Clarity
3. Commitment
The three "C's" equals champion outcomes.

What is your action plan to become the greatest version of yourself?

_____

_____

_____

_____

_____

_____

_____

_____

_____

Part 4

Blueprint For Student Athlete Success

Chapter 16
Keys To Student Athlete Success

Take your education seriously. You've heard it since you were a little kid that knowledge is power. That statement is true and will remain true for the rest of your life. Learn as much as you can in a wide variety of topics. Just remember that "specialized" knowledge is what will add tremendous value in your career.

Specialized knowledge comes from knowing the intricate details of what you want to do. Whatever it is that you want to do, gain as much specialized education as you possibly can in that industry. Formal education at your current school, hopefully, can assist you in that specialized learning. Regardless of the fact, going to school and taking your classes seriously will strengthen your *disciplined* skill set.

I'm sure you and I both can agree that going to school every single day presents its challenges. It's not always easy. One thing that it does help create, again, is **self-discipline.** Another reason to take your education seriously is if you don't have passing grades you will not be eligible to play your sport. Having passing grades and achieving eligibility status is critical towards your entire athletic career. **What good is it to train year round and to have aspirations of playing at the highest level, if you have poor grades that ultimately make you not eligible to play that season?** All it takes is one quarter or semester of not being focused and not passing your classes to hurt your future.

You hold the power. You have control. You get the opportunity every day to show up, to be attentive in class, to give quality effort, and to do the work to be successful with your homework and tests. So much of success, or lack thereof, is *preparation*. **Get prepared, and stay prepared so you're always ready when the opportunity comes to showcase your intelligence and talent. And that goes for the classroom, on the field, and in your life.**

Take networking seriously, especially for readers in college. The relationships you develop and cultivate at this time in your life, right now, will have a major impact in your life years from now. People help people. When you see a successful person just know they had other people help get them to the top. This goes for any and every industry. Always treat people with respect. Look them in the eye. Give them a firm handshake. Have good manners. Do thoughtful things. Always bring your A game! Give others the best you. First impressions mean a lot. First impressions leave a lasting impression. What do you want your legacy to be in the minds of others?

Time Management skills are essential. Create goals and action plans. There is a saying, "If you fail to plan, you plan to fail." Plan your months, your weeks, your days, and even plan your hours. With time management comes organization. In order to be a productive person, you need time management skills.

R.E.P. - Reverse Engineer Program

Start with the end in mind and work your way backwards. The REP program is especially important in the visualization process. REP with visualization is a creative process. You may not currently be where you want to be, but you have the power to envision in your mind who you want to become and all the details of what your future life looks like. That's seeing the end in mind. Now you have to work backwards to get clarity on the steps that it will take to reach that end vision. This goes for the person you want to become, the dreams you envision achieving, and anything that your imagination can conceive.

This whole book is your guide to student athlete success. Allow the words in this book to help you along your journey with:

- Creating your own success as an athlete
- Empowering yourself to meet your goals
- Going deep within to bring outer excellence
- Becoming who you want to be

R.E.P.

Your Vision

Reverse Engineer Program Your Vision

Chapter 17
Successful Communication & Positioning

In order to get what you want, you need to *align* yourself with the right people. What do I mean by this? Think about your end goal in mind. What results do you want? Whatever this vision is, you cannot achieve it solely on your own. You should seek out the individuals or groups of people that have already accomplished what it is that you want to accomplish, and have them be your mentor. Learn from them. Study them. This is what I mean when I use the word, "alignment."

Aligning yourself with other people who can help you is obviously important, but an even more important step is first aligning with your inner self. Align with your core values. Are your outer actions an appropriate reflection of what's going on inside? If what you're doing is not in alignment with your heart, you'll have struggles. You have to find that balance between what your heart is telling you to do, what you're thinking, and what you're doing.

Heart. Mind. Action.

Being able to articulate and communicate effectively is important. Make sure your goals, your actions, and your daily habits all support your desired end result. That's true, purposeful positioning. *Demonstrate what you want by what you do.*

Ask questions whenever you need clarification. Asking questions is a sign of someone who values learning. It also demonstrates that you appreciate what the other person is talking about. Ask questions often. When teachers and professors know that you are an attentive student, and you demonstrate the *want* to learn more through your questions, they will respect you on a deeper scholastic level. Bringing your A game to the classroom, coupled with seeking more knowledge through questions, will have a dramatic impact on your teacher to student relationship. Which in return will pay off in a major way down the line if and when you need their support for any reason.

Our education system is highly based off of your performance with homework and tests. But I'm here to tell you right now that there is an X factor. That X factor can be summed up in one word. ***Effort***. Have you ever had a class where the teacher grades you on participation? Take full advantage of participation points. Consistently give effort.

When you've taken the time to further enhance and cultivate a relationship with your teacher, and you've consistently demonstrated putting forth effort with your education, that plays a part in the grading scale. It will have a positive impact on your academic success.

DEEP Reflection

The best communicators are great listeners. Always *listen with intent* and apply what you learn. How can you improve your communication skills? Do you need to become a better intentful listener? Start now.

Chapter 18
Prehab Training

Rehab is reactive. Prehab is proactive. In our strength training for our sport, just like in life, being proactive makes the difference. While training in the weight room, we work out the major muscle groups. The smart thing to do is to also strengthen and train the smaller muscle groups and tendons. For example, doing leg extensions help strengthen the smaller muscles that protect your knee, doing different shoulder exercises using band resistance training strengthens the smaller ligaments that protect your shoulder. Since we do prehab training in the weight room and with our workouts, shouldn't we also prehab train our minds for success in life? The answer is ABSOLUTELY! The prehab training for our mind helps enhance our habits, decision-making, and the direction we go in life, which all ultimately elevates our life experiences.

Don't wait to get hurt to do rehab. Lessen the chances of preventable injuries by doing prehab and strengthening the necessary areas of your body. The same goes for your everyday life. Don't wait for adversity to strike to see if you overcome the storm. Don't wait for challenging times to test your willpower and resilience. Do the prehab training for *life* now. Strengthen your mind, elevate your mindset, enhance your attitude, and shift your perspective in more optimistic ways that will impact you now and for future events.

Along your journey, always *prevent what's preventable* and *prepare* so that when sudden change happens you're mentally equipped to handle it.

Chapter 19
Get Involved

I was very blessed and I feel so honored
to have played football at the Ohio State
University. It is one the best academic
institutions in the country and the best
football program in the country.
Throughout history, Ohio State has had
some incredible coaches. One in
particular was Coach Woody Hayes. He
stressed the importance of **paying it
forward**. He laid the foundation of
encouraging student athletes to get
involved with the community and give
back to youth and patients in need at
hospitals. My head coach, Coach Jim
Tressel, 100% followed the foundation
of paying it forward that was laid by
Coach Hayes. There's really 2 main parts
to this chapter, "*Get involved*". The first
message is to remind athletes of the
tremendous platform that they have.
Their voices get heard, and their voices
make an impact in the millions upon
millions of sports fans around the world.

I'm here to remind the athletes and to
encourage them to use this powerful
platform to be of service and to give
back to their communities. It's an

amazing experience to see a young child suffering from an illness receive a visit from a player representing their favorite sports team. It not only impacts the child. It also lifts the spirits of their parents, friends, and family. It is also an amazing experience to see the youth light up with smiles and give their undivided *attention* to the athlete that comes to their school to read books to them, and give them words of encouragement. I've witnessed it firsthand through the leadership of Coach Tressel and I've had countless "Thank Yous" from Ohio State supporters who appreciate what my teammates have done. It truly does make a difference! Whether you are a current athlete right now or not.... how can you give back to your community? What can you do to make a positive impact in the lives of those around you? I urge you to answer those questions, and then to go out and be of service.

That's part 1.

Part 2 is about getting involved with school organizations, leadership conferences, and leadership trainings. Take advantage of any and all opportunities that your school offers you that involves leadership development. Student athletes have such busy schedules year round that it can be a challenge to participate in activities outside of their chosen sport, but it is possible. It is doable. I know it's possible because I did it. I'm a much better person because I did it. It's a special experience going to a college leadership conference where you have hundreds of other student athletes and coaches there who are representatives of their schools. The lessons learned, the knowledge shared, and the wisdom gained is impeccable. I was fortunate to have administration at Ohio State that deeply cared about the further development of the student athlete as a whole person. People like Coach Jim Tressel, Athletic Director Gene Smith, and amazing counselors at the Student Athlete Success Center played a critical role in not only allowing players to get involved, but they did a phenomenal job in *encouraging* their student athletes to get involved.

Do you have a relationship with your administration at your school? If not, build one. Develop a relationship with your athletic director, counselors, and the support staff that are there to help you as a student athlete. These people will be paramount in your journey of further life skills training and networking opportunities. Again, I say get involved. First you have to want to do "a thing". Then you have to go pursue it. I'll leave you with this. Just because there are opportunities to get involved with organizations and conference trainings (which are great for future resumes) they're not just handed to you. Just like I had to do, you have to seek out those opportunities on purpose. You have to ask questions about what opportunities are available to you. And then you have to apply. There's a process. The opportunities are there. It's up to you as a motivated individual to take advantage of the opportunities to get involved, and be an honorable representation of the school you represent.

Here are your options for ways you can get involved.
- ❖ Ask yourself how you can serve your local community.
- ❖ Go to the resource center at school. Ask a teacher or coach. There is someone in close

proximity to you that can lead you in the right direction to get involved in community service and to also network.

❖ For college student athletes, here are a few programs and conferences to apply for.

- NCAA National Leadership Conference
- NCAA Champs Life Skills Program
- SAAB (Student Athlete Advisory Board)
- SAAC (Student Athlete Advisory Committee)
- Apple Conference (Drug and Alcohol Leadership Conference)

One last thing I will leave you with in this chapter is to be creative and consider joining, or starting your own student organization.

I had an idea in college that became the 1,000[th] recognized student organization. It was called, Strike The Mic. The whole premise was for players to interview players and talk about topics outside of sports so the fans could get to know us better. I shared the concept with a few of my teammates and Strike The Mic quickly gained momentum. Teammates DeVier Posey, Nate Oliver, Chimdi Checkwa Dan Bain, Terrelle Pryor, Spencer Smith, Jordan Whiting, Tony Jackson and Jamie Wood were several guys that saw the vision and got involved.

Coach Tressel supported the idea of Strike The Mic and participated in a commercial with myself and other teammates.

Ohio State's then President, Dr. Gordon Gee also embraced Strike The Mic and had me tour with him for his state wide appearance tour! I would interview Dr. Gee along different stops of the tour, and at times speak to large crowds that came out to support the tour and the University.

Through networking and asking for help I was even able to meet President Obama and First Lady, Michelle Obama when they came to Ohio State's campus and addressed thousands of people at the Oval in the heart of the campus!

I was extremely fortunate and blessed to have my coach, administration and president of the University's support in helping me launch my Strike The Mic which helped my teammates and I get first hand experience in leadership, media, marketing and communication skills.

You too can create and attract opportunities into your life by taking action with your vision. **Go create and have the full student athlete experience by getting INVOLVED.**

Part 5

Redshirt
to
Whiteshirt

Chapter 20
Moving On To
Different Playing Fields

One thing that is constant in life is change. A lot of times "change" can feel *uncomfortable* and scary. But when you know that change is going to happen, you can be a little more prepared for when it comes.

I transferred to Huber Heights Wayne High School in January of my sophomore year. Being a Wayne Warrior was vastly different. Like I mentioned early in the book, the workouts, training regime, and expectation were extremely high.

Demonstrate leadership and work ethic consistently in the weight room, studies and make sure to cultivate relationships and develop trust. Nothing will be handed to you. Even if you have an edge and hype around your name, you have to prove day in and day out why you deserve your desired success.

The challenges to moving on to different playing fields are not going to be easy. It's going to present its obstacles, but it will also present opportunities. You, as an athlete, are use to routine. You know when you have classes, practice, games, etc.... There's a structure. From morning to night your schedule is accounted for. So when it's over and you're transitioning, you're now 100% responsible for yourself.

You don't have coaches, teachers, counselors, or tutors looking over your shoulder. There's no one looking over you. You have to be mature enough to take all the skills that you've learned and transfer that.

When your playing career is over one of the toughest things to transition from, and one thing most athletes miss is the camaraderie. You're so used to being with your team. Now you've all graduated and you don't have that daily interaction. Now if you don't go to the NFL, what happens when you come back home? You will go through a mental transition. It may be positive or depressing.

You're so used to playing sports. You might feel freedom. Or you might feel depression because things didn't turn out the way you thought it would. The key is to find healthy ways to cope with the emotions you experience post-sports. It's imperative to have a healthy outlet because you can quickly find yourself at the bars and clubs more often than not. You're still you. You're still the athlete. Now you're going to grow different parts of who you are. Whatever you move on to with your career and life you need to apply the same disciplines that made you successful in between the white lines. Apply the same method, strategies and work ethic that made you successful in your sport. Take those same things and apply it from the playing field to your new career field in whatever you choose to do.

You wouldn't believe how tough it can be to move from playing something you loved. It's something every young man and young lady must do. But how? How does a person who has dedicated so much time and spent the majority of their life playing successfully move on? I'm still learning. What I can advise is that you reflect inwardly. Don't just reflect on a surface level. Look deep within yourself and search what you are passionate about.

Chapter 21
Tackling Transition

❖ What To Expect

What's the difference between quitting and transitioning? Quitting is giving up and not having a plan. Transitioning is more like a pivot, moving in a different direction with a *game plan*. You've got to look in the mirror and have a one on one with yourself. You need a goal setting session with yourself to be your own accountability partner.

Every level of transcendence will present some degree of culture shock. For example, middle school to high school, high school to college, college to professional, and then from your last play as an athlete to transitioning to the "real world". Know this. Realize this. Awareness is key. Internalizing what I'm conveying to you will help you be more prepared only for what's destined to happen.

❖ **Transferable Skills**

Your skills as a student athlete are transferable. Articulate them. These are things that are transferrable
- Being able to work in a team environment
- Good work ethic
- Punctuality
- Perseverance
- Positive attitude
- Commitment
- Goal-oriented
- Self-driven
- Communication skills
- Being dedicated

Realize that you have a lot to offer. What you've learned through being a competitive athlete will greatly benefit you in your endeavors as an entrepreneur and/or the job you choose.

Photo of Nathan Baker and I rehearsing for Dayton's ABC22
Fox45 The Road To The Big Game Live Show, Ohio State vs
Michigan 2013. Nathan gave me my 1st opportunity at Live TV.

Covering the 2014 National Championship Game with Erik Elken and the man who handles the behind the scenes work, Mr. Larry. (Photo below) is my former Ohio State teammate and I on Good Day Columbus talking Buckeye Football just 48 hours before the National Championship Game OSU vs Oregon

On Set with The Best Damn Band In The Land!

Press Box view of over 105,000 people storming the field after Ohio State beats Michigan in Overtime 2016 30 to 27!

Watching the 4th quarter and Overtime with legendary former Ohio State Coach, Earl Bruce...Priceless! His smile says it all! Go Bucks!

Chapter 22
Life After Sports

There's a grief in closing this chapter of your life. Hanging up your jersey can feel like the death of an athlete. I want to help this transition be as smooth and as healthy as possible. I want to encourage you to transfer these applicable athletic skills to life after sports.

Coming from someone who is done playing sports and has moved on, I'm here to let you know that the majority of your former teammates are experiencing similar emotions and feelings with adjusting to life after sports. **Take initiative and don't solo tackle this transition phase**. In football the defense is taught to pursue the ball. Eleven guys are hustling and giving full 100% effort to make the tackle together as a defensive unit. Yes, there are plenty of times in a football game where a guy will get a solo tackle, but there are plenty of times where you see 3 or 4 guys make the play together. So, take that same approach when the game is over. Tackle the rough times together by locking arms and being a genuine friend and true teammate. And pursue the great opportunities that present themselves to former athletes. Share opportunities. From my experience, doors have opened for my teammates and I simply because we played for a prestigious football program like Ohio State, and created a quality reputation and brand for ourselves.

The fact of the matter is, the majority of people respect (and in a way look up to) sports figures. So, look forward to opportunities presenting themselves to you even if you stopped playing in high school or if you happen to play at a smaller school in college. The fact remains you will have opportunities within your alumni and your school's community because you were a part of their team. Tackle your future experiences with your teammates.

Coach Tressel, Storm Klein, Nate Oliver and myself attending an "Ohio Fallen Heroes" event, honoring the Men and Woman who serve our Country. Coach Tressel would always remind his players that Freedom isn't free. Thank you to all the men, women and their families who serve our great country!

Photo of former OSU student athletes, professional athletes and professional business people at the Complete Athlete Program. Ohio State's leaders are launching programs that will help every student athlete that comes through the University! Several former players in this photo are Chim Checkwa, Malcolm Jenkins, Eddie George, Raymont Harris and Dallas Lauderdale.

Myself, and one of Ohio State's great kickers Tim Williams, along with former Cincinnati Bengal Ira Hillary visiting Dayton Childrens Hospital with Santa. Myself and my teammates have done countless hospital visits. Each time it feels amazing to help put a smile on the face of a child and their family!

Chapter 23
Tackling With
TEAMMATES

Teams that achieve great success harness the power of the unit. Coaches and players come together for one common goal. Each individual player puts energy and effort to be the best at their position and the best at their craft. When individuals have the hunger and the work ethic to be the best, that collectively makes everyone around them better. Players rely on other teammates to have a successful play, to have a successful series, to have a successful game, and to have a successful season. The same applies for life after sports. Teammates still need each other. Men and women need to maintain and enhance the relationships that they had with their high school, college, and professional teammates. During the playing days teammates create priceless memories, amazing experiences, bonds through brotherhood and sisterhood that can last a lifetime. The transition into the real world can be challenging, but having teammates that you played with still having your back and you having theirs makes the transition process that much better. You don't feel as alone. You feel like you can do more with the support and encouraging words from your brothers and sisters who've been to battle with you on the field.

The people who've been on sports teams that are reading this may have a deeper understanding of the message that I'm conveying. You once relied on each other during competitive sports. You can still rely on each other in the competitive business world. Tackle life with teammates. Be the lead block for your teammate when he needs help. And hit the hole hard when your teammate creates a lane of opportunity for you. Remember this. The ups and downs that you may experience when sports are over are very similar to the feelings and emotions that your teammates will experience as well. Our careers as athletes may end at different times (for one person their last play may be college, another's last play was high school, and another player might have been a professional), but once it's all said and done you will always be teammates with those you once shared the competitive field with.

Reach out and connect with teammates you played with. Also reach out to guys that came years before you. Take pride in being an alumni and connect with other alumni members to create more lasting memories for your life moving forward.

My Buckeye Brothers Nate Oliver, Will Allen, Jay Richardson and myself at the After School All Stars ceremony during The Arnold Classic weekend, in Columbus Ohio. Each one of us believes strongly in paying it forward with our time and platform we've been blessed with.

Part 6

Applying Athletic Alchemy

Chapter 24
Checklist For Success

- ✓ Use the S.T.O.P. technique.
- ✓ Maximize the intangibles.
- ✓ Mastering your mind equals mastering your life.
- ✓ Create your ID.
- ✓ Use the REP program
- ✓ Know who you are.
- ✓ Know your number.
- ✓ Stay humble.
- ✓ Stay hungry.
- ✓ Utilize deep affirmations.
- ✓ Tackle temptations head on.
- ✓ Overcome obstacles.
- ✓ Ask for help.
- ✓ Time management skills are critical for success.
- ✓ Create healthy outlets.
- ✓ Persevere a little bit longer and a little bit harder. You may be closer than you think to achieving your dreams.
- ✓ Ramp up your ambition!
- ✓ Show up!
- ✓ Remember that YOU are a Brand.
- ✓ It's bigger than just you. Remember what You Represent.
- ✓ Don't self-sabotage.
- ✓ Excuses will kill your greatness.

✓ Self-discipline is vital.
✓ Invest in yourself.
✓ Value and take your education seriously.
✓ Network and get involved as often as possible.
✓ Effective communication (be an intentional listener).
✓ Effort
✓ Prevent what is preventable i.e. prehab training
✓ One of the first things coaches at the next level want to know is, "Does this athlete have high character, does he/she work hard in the classroom and weight room? Do your part so the coaches know the answer is always, YES!

When you do these things you are *positioning* yourself for greatness. Do them. Check them. Repeat.

Chapter 25
Applying This To Your Life

For all you student athletes, professional athletes, and anyone else reading this book: remember, it will only work once you internalize this material and *apply it to your life*. Application and **execution** are really the only things that matter. You have the ability to get better results and achieve your dreams! It's up to You to take action.

You have everything *within* to experience outer excellence in every area of your life!

-Go DEEP-

OTHER BOOKS BY THIS AUTHOR

Make sure to get Donnie's first book,

The Deep Journal

The DEEP Journal was created for you to empower your life. You have potential inside you that's just waiting to be released to the world! Your dreams, visions, and goals are waiting to come to fruition. What's holding you back from achieving your goals? One way to find out the reason "why" is through writing. In this journal, you'll be given a mental technique that will empower you to be proactive in striving towards your dreams, and becoming the Best YOU possible.

Contact

For speaking engagements, workshop trainings and appearances, contact Donnie through his website www.DonnieRayEvege.com

CONNECT WITH THE AUTHOR

Stay in contact via all social media accounts:

Facebook, Instagram, Youtube, Twitter
@DonnieRayEvege

A major key in life is to show gratitude and appreciation to those who have taken time out of their lives to help you along your journey.

THANK YOU

Writing this book has been a process. There are people I'd like to thank for helping and encouraging me during this journey.

To My Mom, Chrissy Evege

When I was down and out you helped lift me up. When I questioned life, you reminded me of my purpose and meaning. When I wanted to quit and give in, you inspired me to win personal battles. You are My Rock! I can't Thank You enough for the unconditional support, encouragement, love, and lessons you've instilled and shared with me. This book is dedicated to the millions of student athletes around the world... but it's because of YOU that it was written.

I Love You, Mom!

To My Dad, Donnie Ray Evege Sr.

I could write an entire book about the wonderful father, and amazing role model you've been to myself and many young men! I appreciate you from the bottom of my heart. If it were not for the sacrifices You and Mom made, there's no way I would have been in a position to showcase my talent and receive a scholarship to a D1 school. Thank You! You've taught me through your actions what it means to be a Courageous Man of Faith. You've taught me the importance of having sportsmanship, and you taught me the importance of hard work and planning for the future. It's because of You that I put pen to paper and wrote out my goals and followed through. You are the Best Dad I could ask for, and a 2nd to none Coach myself and your players could have asked for. Thank You, Dad!

I Love You, Dad!

To My Sister, Briana Evege

Thank You for always being by my side and in my corner! You've made so many sacrifices growing up and I appreciate everything you do. You've been an incredible sister, and now an amazing mother. I love you, my niece Soraya, nephew Ryder, Baby Number Three on the way and Charles very much!

You're a beautiful person inside and out and I'm blessed to have you as my sister!!!

I Love You!

To my book coach, Leanna Mae Sexton

Thank you for the support, advice, sacrifice and time you dedicated to this book! You are a true professional, and a great friend. Thank you for helping Athletic Alchemy come alive.
www.LeannaMae.org

Coach Jim Tressel

A very special thank you goes to the man who believed in me, and gave me a priceless opportunity to be a part of the best college football program in history, a man who gave me the blessing of an opportunity to receive my education from an incredible university, and a man who allowed me time to be coached and mentored by him; Coach Jim Tressel.

A selfless and purpose driven coach who deeply cares for and loves his players. A coach who instilled values and spiritual faith in his team. A man who made it a priority to encourage his players to be well-rounded men to become leaders in life. A man who allowed and encouraged me to get involved in leadership committees, student organization, and community outreaches.

A man who is a father figure, and a Champion Coach.

Coach Tressel, THANK YOU!!

Singing Carmen Ohio after a victory at Ohio Stadium.
Priceless memories with priceless people.

Thank You Buckeye Nation.
You are Incredible fans!

Salute to you!

Visit my website
www.DonnieRayEvege.com to view
extended "Thank You" list.

Last but not least I want to **THANK YOU**, the reader! Thank You for taking the time to read my book. I pray something in this book helps you along your journey.

Use Athletic Alchemy to help *transform* your life.

Always remember to

Go DEEP Within To Bring Outer Excellence